PRESERVED
Vegetables

VOLUME 4

PRESERVED

Vegetables

DARRA GOLDSTEIN / CORTNEY BURNS / RICHARD MARTIN

PHOTOGRAPHY BY DAVID MALOSH

Hardie Grant
NORTH AMERICA

CONTENTS

- **1** The Transformative Power of Vegetables
- **30** The Blue Goddess
- **99** Notes on Ingredients
- **101** Notes on Equipment
- **102** Index
- **104** Acknowledgments

RECIPES

- 7 Butternut Squash and Sesame Purée
- 8 Fermented Winter Squash
- 11 Golden Cabbage
- 12 Sauerkraut Three Ways
- 16 Carrot and Barberry Salad
- 21 Charred Baba Ghanoush
- 22 Fermented Eggplant
- 25 Eggplant Makdous
- 27 Ajvar
- 33 Zesty Asparagus Pickles
- 34 Cucumbers Brined in a Pumpkin
- 38 Pickled Gazpacho with Charred Tomatoes and Peppers
- 41 Tangy Corn on the Cob
- 42 Warm Corn Relish
- 47 Sweet Corn Tea
- 48 Vinegret
- 52 Vegetable Fritters
- 53 Fermented Whole Vegetables
- 57 Misozuke
- 58 Duck Fat Steak Fries
- 60 Cauliflower-Turmeric Pickle
- 65 Marinated Mushrooms Two Ways
- 69 Sambal-Style Chile Pepper Paste
- 70 Fire-Roasted and Oil-Preserved Peppers
- 73 Cheese-Stuffed Roasted Peppers
- 74 Pickled Cherry Tomatoes
- 76 Pickled Cherry Tomato and Ricotta Tart
- 80 Tomato Water
- 83 Green Tomato Marmalade
- 84 Mixed Vegetable Tzimmes
- 87 Beet and Carrot Eingemacht
- 88 Dongchimi
- 91 Pumpkin Candy
- 95 Homemade Paprika

The Transformative Power of Vegetables

The ability of vegetables to transform, and to be transformed, is what might be called their superpower.

The admonition to "eat your vegetables" as part of a healthy diet is a modern-day concept, a long-simmering result of centuries-old agricultural development and experimentation. Though vegetables have been a source of nourishment for eons, dating back to the time of hunter-gatherers, they were given their English name as a category of food only in the late sixteenth century.

The ability of vegetables to transform, and to be transformed, is what might be called their superpower. In this volume, we coax flavors, colors, and textures out of vegetables through pickling, fermentation, sugaring, and dehydrating, while also exploring the full range of vegetables' malleability and versatility. The recipes reflect not only time-tested techniques to preserve eggplant, butternut squash, and asparagus, to name a few of today's vegetable all-stars, but ideas for new preparations that will have you remixing and reimagining your seasonal produce.

Taking the idea of metamorphosis farther, consider this: many of the vegetables that exist as we know them today are inventions, the results of crossbreeding, hybridization, and the work of what the food writer Jane Grigson has referred to as "enterprising seedsmen." In the seventeenth century, Dutch horticulturists bred carrots—originally yellow and purple (sometimes called "black") when they were first domesticated—into the familiar orange hue found today. The modern variety of butternut squash originated only in 1944, when Charles Leggett of Stow, Massachusetts, crossed pumpkin and gooseneck squash—both perfectly acceptable on their own, but certainly not as tasty when turned into a soup, a purée, or our fermented winter squash dip (page 8). Beets are also a case study in transformation. Originally cultivated on Mediterranean coastlines for their edible leaves and stalks, in the sixteenth century they began to be more widely grown throughout Europe for their roots as well. By the 1700s, Prussians had developed a long, pointed, white variety that came to be known as the sugar beet. Scientists selectively bred the beets for sugar content and created a method to extract the sugar, and today, sugar beets grown and harvested to produce sucrose account for nearly a third of the world's supply of table sugar.

This is all something to think about when visiting your local farmers' market—itself one of a multitude that, powered by vegetables, enrich communities and help maintain the role of small farmers in our food system. Vegetables serve as driving forces and tools for innovation across wide swaths of our society. Corn-derived ethanol helps lower carbon dioxide emissions from gas-powered vehicles. Companies producing plant-based meat alternatives manipulate vegetable proteins and beet juice to produce burgers, nuggets, and sausages that mimic the taste and texture of beef, chicken, and pork. Mycelium, the rootlike system of mushrooms, is the basis of a plant-based alternative to leather. Humans' use of vegetables beyond simply growing and eating them isn't a new phenomenon. Textile makers and other artisans have long employed vegetable dyes to add color to rugs, clothing, and other fabrics, as we explore on page 30.

Vegetables are gaining new importance right now as part of their latest progression: from side dish to primary ingredient. The environmental and health benefits of eating your vegetables—especially to replace or reduce consumption of both meat and heavily processed foods—are now accepted as fact in our culture. Decades of research show that eating five or more servings of fruits and vegetables per day reduces blood pressure and lowers the risks of heart disease and cancer. Carotenoids, the organic pigments that give color to orange, yellow, and red vegetables, also provide natural antioxidants.

Our renewed sense of vegetables' value brings us back to preservation. While vegetables are unquestionably nutritious, their short shelf life requires either near-immediate use or some method to maximize their staying power. Fortunately for us, enterprising humans across cultures and through time have developed ingenious preservation techniques: fermenting cabbage gives us kimchi and sauerkraut; cucumbers mixed with herbs, spices, and vinegar become dill pickles; tomatoes dried by the sun can reemerge in dishes weeks or months later, their flavor intensified. What was ephemeral becomes long-lasting.

The recipes that follow go far beyond the building blocks of vegetable preservation to reveal the transformational potential of every part of a vegetable. Corn and its silk ferment with chile pepper to create a base for a warm corn relish (page 42); the cobs are brewed with black tea, lemon verbena, blueberries, and honey for a mesmerizing sweet tea (page 47). Eggplant takes an unexpected journey, from roasting to puréeing to fermenting, on its way to becoming charred, fermented baba ghanoush (page 21). And for those of you who like to turn up the heat, you'll learn how to ferment chile peppers in the style of Indonesian sambal (page 69) and to make the Balkan red pepper spread known as ajvar (page 27).

We love fresh vegetables, of course, but in creating the recipes for this volume of *Preserved*, we hope to share our conviction that preservation is a pathway to both reinvention and discovery, with flavors that will electrify—and perhaps even transform—your taste buds.

MAKES ABOUT 3 CUPS *or* 720 MILLILITERS

Butternut Squash and Sesame Purée

Fermented winter squash is a key ingredient in this powerhouse purée, which layers flavor upon flavor to create a versatile addition to your cold-season larder. It can be presented as a side dish, used to add depth to soups and pastas, or slathered on grilled bread for a savory starter. We especially like to serve this purée as a dip topped with toasted pumpkin seeds and pumpkin-seed oil—a sophisticated and delicious play on the pumpkin-spice frenzy of late fall and early winter. To achieve a smooth, silky texture, first blitz in a food processor to break down the vegetables and combine them with the other ingredients, then transfer to a blender to finish the purée, working in batches if necessary.

12 ounces / 340 g fresh winter squash, such as kabocha or butternut
10 ounces / 280 g Fermented Winter Squash (page 8)
2 ounces / 56 g sweet potato
3 garlic cloves, peeled and stem ends removed
¼ cup / 64 g tahini
1½ tablespoons white miso
2 tablespoons freshly squeezed lemon juice
1 teaspoon kosher salt
1¼ teaspoons ground coriander
½ teaspoon ground cumin
¼ teaspoon ground turmeric
⅛ teaspoon ground black pepper
⅛ teaspoon ground ginger
½ teaspoon onion powder
½ teaspoon fennel pollen (or use ¼ teaspoon each aniseed and fennel seed, toasted and ground)
¾ teaspoon hot paprika or ground cayenne pepper
½ teaspoon freshly grated lemon zest
2 tablespoons brine from Fermented Winter Squash (page 8)
¼ cup / 60 ml extra-virgin olive oil
Toasted pumpkin seeds (optional), for garnish
Roasted pumpkin seed oil (optional), for garnish

Peel the fresh squash and sweet potato and cut them into 1-inch / 2.5 cm chunks. Fill a large pot with 1 to 2 inches / 2.5 to 5 cm of water and fit a steamer basket inside, making sure the water isn't high enough to seep into the basket. Cover the pot and bring to a gentle simmer over medium heat. Steam the fresh and fermented squash, sweet potato, and garlic together, covered, until they are soft enough to mash, about 20 minutes. Remove the pot from the heat and leave to cool for about 10 minutes.

Transfer the vegetables to the bowl of a food processor and pulse a few times to break them up slightly. Add the tahini, miso, lemon juice, salt, spices, zest, and brine and continue to process until smooth. With the processor still running, slowly stream in the oil to make a silky, emulsified purée. Let cool to room temperature and taste for seasoning, adding more salt if desired. Transfer to an airtight container and refrigerate. The purée will keep for 2 to 3 weeks.

To serve as a dip, spoon the purée into a bowl and garnish with toasted pumpkin seeds and pumpkin seed oil.

MAKES ABOUT 1 QUART *or* 1 LITER

Fermented Winter Squash

Unlike fermented vegetables that retain some of their crispness, this squash isn't intended for nibbling. Instead, the recipe yields a soft fermented squash that is perfectly suited for making purées or blending into soups. For this recipe, you'll make a 3.5 percent brine, with a weight of kosher salt added to water in proportion to the water's weight; see the Salt entry on page 99 for details.

1 (2-pound / 900 g) winter squash, such as butternut, kabocha, or Hubbard
Kosher salt, for brine

Sterilize a 1-quart / 1 L canning jar or fermentation crock. Peel the squash, then slice it in half and remove the seeds. Cut it into 1- to 2-inch / 2.5 to 5 cm chunks and place them in the jar. Pour in enough water to completely cover the squash. As you do, keep track of how much water you add, since this will dictate the amount of salt you need. Calculate 3.5 percent of the weight of the water used and measure out that amount of kosher salt. Stir the salt into the water in the jar with a long wooden spoon until the salt is dissolved (or add the salt, cap the jar, and shake well).

Place a weight or small saucer on top of the squash to keep it submerged in the brine. Seal the container, using a lid with an airlock if you have one; if you don't, open the container every few days to release carbon dioxide buildup and check for mold (if any has accumulated, you can gently scrape off). Place the container in a low-light area with an ambient temperature of 60°F to 68°F / 16°C to 20°C for about 3 weeks, until the brine is opaque and the squash tastes sour. Transfer the pickles in their brine to the refrigerator, where they will keep indefinitely.

MAKES ABOUT 2 QUARTS *or* 2 LITERS

Golden Cabbage

This fermented cabbage is made without hot peppers, so it has a gentler taste than most kimchi. The lack of fieriness allows the flavors of bell peppers and saffron to shine through, and the cabbage takes on a lovely golden hue.

- 2 pounds / 900 g Napa cabbage hearts, large outer green leaves removed
- 2 quarts / 2 L water
- 1 cup plus 3 tablespoons / 171 g kosher salt
- 2 ice cubes
- 4 to 6 saffron threads, ground to a powder in a mortar
- ½ cup / 90 g jasmine rice
- 1½ pounds / 680 g yellow or orange bell peppers, stemmed, seeded, and chopped
- ½ pound / 225 g daikon, tops removed, peeled, and chopped
- ½ pound / 225 g Asian pear or apple, peeled, cored, and chopped
- 1 (1-inch / 2.5 cm) knob of ginger, peeled and thinly sliced
- 3 garlic cloves, coarsely chopped

Wash the cabbage hearts thoroughly under cold running water and remove any damaged or wilted leaves. Cut the cabbage hearts lengthwise in half or in quarters without removing the cores and place the pieces in a large bowl.

Mix 1 quart / 1 L of the water with 1 cup / 144 g of the salt, stirring well to combine, then pour the salt water over the cabbage. Place a small plate on top of the cabbage to weigh it down and leave it submerged in the brine at room temperature, turning it once or twice, until wilted, at least 3 hours and up to overnight.

When the cabbage is wilted, place the ice cubes in a small bowl and sprinkle the ground saffron over them. Let sit at room temperature until the ice is fully melted.

Preheat the oven to 375°F / 190°C. Pour the rice onto a small baking tray and smooth it into a single layer. Toast for 12 to 15 minutes, until golden and fragrant. Bring the remaining 1 quart / 1 L of water to a boil in a medium saucepan. Add the toasted rice, reduce the heat, and simmer, uncovered, for 10 minutes. Drain the rice over a large bowl to catch the water, then measure out 1½ cups / 360 ml of the rice water (don't discard the rest; you may need it). Set aside to cool.

In a blender, combine the bell peppers, daikon, Asian pear, ginger, and garlic, and pour in the saffron water. Blend until the ingredients are puréed, then set a fine-mesh sieve lined with cheesecloth over a bowl. Drain well, squeezing the cheesecloth to release the last bit of liquid. You should have about 3 cups / 720 ml of liquid. Combine this with the 1½ cups / 360 ml of rice water to yield 4½ cups / 1.1 L of liquid total. If you come up short, add some reserved rice water. Stir in the remaining 3 tablespoons / 27 g of kosher salt.

Remove the cabbage from the salt brine and rinse it under cold water, wringing it out gently with your hands. Pack the cabbage into a sterilized 2-quart / 2 L canning jar and pour the liquid over the cabbage, then place a sterilized weight on the cabbage to keep it submerged. Cover the jar tightly and leave the cabbage to ferment at room temperature (68°F to 72°F / 20°C to 22°C) for 5 to 10 days or more, depending on how sour you like it, briefly opening and closing the lid daily to release trapped carbon dioxide. Once the cabbage has achieved the flavor you like, store it in the refrigerator, where it will last for 6 months or more.

Sauerkraut Three Ways
Sauerkraut Soup, Apple Kraut, Sauerkraut Powder

SAUERKRAUT SOUP
MAKES ABOUT 3 QUARTS / 3 L

Sauerkraut soup is enjoyed throughout Central and Eastern Europe, and no wonder— it's one of the best ways to fortify yourself against winter's cold. This recipe takes its inspiration from the Polish version, bigos, *in which the base ingredient is cabbage— fresh, salted, or a mixture of both. But it skews slightly Hungarian in its inclusion of hot paprika and caraway seed and of fire-roasted tomatoes.*

Bigos was once reserved for the aristocracy, which is not surprising given the amount of meat it contains. The dish came to be associated with hunting, a pastime forbidden to the hoi polloi. During the hunt, bigos was prepared in an iron cauldron hung over an open fire. Bigos is said to taste best after it's been reheated three times and was also considered ideal travelers' fare.

Over time, bigos was democratized, so that it's now as likely to be served in pubs as at banquets. Also, the ingredients are now mixed together rather than layered as they once were. But the belief that bigos should be thick has endured. We make ours thinner than the stand-up-your-spoon Polish version, but you should feel free to play around with the amount of chicken broth you add. Rustic rye bread and ice-cold vodka are favored accompaniments.

- 1 pound / 454 g boneless pork shoulder, cut into 1-inch / 2.5 cm chunks
- Kosher salt and freshly ground black pepper
- 3 to 4 tablespoons neutral oil, such as grapeseed or light olive oil
- ¼ cup / 60 ml dry white wine
- 1 pound / 454 g smoked kielbasa, sliced into ½-inch / 1.25 cm coins
- 4 ounces / 115 g slab bacon, cut into small dice
- 2 sweet white onions, cut into large dice
- 8 ounces / 225 g button mushrooms, stemmed, and halved or quartered depending on size
- 2 green serrano chiles, thinly sliced
- 2 red bell peppers, stemmed, seeded, and cut into ½-inch / 1.25 cm dice
- 12 garlic cloves, peeled and chopped
- 3 tablespoons hot paprika
- 1½ tablespoons caraway seed
- ¼ teaspoon ground allspice
- 2 tablespoons kosher salt
- 1 (28-ounce / 794 g) can diced fire-roasted tomatoes, and their juice
- 2 bay leaves
- 1 cup / 240 ml sauerkraut brine
- 1½ to 2 quarts / 1.5 to 2 L chicken broth
- ⅓ cup / 60 g pitted, quartered prunes or dried apricots, or whole dried sour cherries
- 3 cups / 415 g drained Apple Kraut (recipe follows) or other sauerkraut
- Sour cream, scallion, and dill, for garnish

Pat the pork dry with a paper towel and season it with salt and pepper. In a large, heavy-bottom Dutch oven or stockpot, heat the oil on medium-high until it shimmers. Add the pork in a single layer and sear it on all sides until golden, 1 to 2 minutes per side. Carefully move the seared pork and rendered fat into a bowl.

Return the pot to the heat and add the wine to deglaze, scraping to release all the flavorful bits from the bottom of the pan. Once the wine has mostly evaporated, add the kielbasa slices and sear them until browned on both sides, then use a slotted spoon to transfer them to a small plate, leaving their rendered fat in the pot.

Add the bacon and cook, stirring occasionally, until it just begins to release its fat, about 5 minutes. CONTINUED ▶

SAUERKRAUT THREE WAYS CONTINUED

Next, add the onions, mushrooms, chiles, and bell peppers. Cook, stirring occasionally, until the onions and peppers begin to soften, 8 to 10 minutes. Add the garlic, paprika, caraway, allspice, and the salt to the pot. Cook for about 3 minutes, until the spices are fragrant.

Add the tomatoes and their juice, the sauerkraut brine, 1½ quarts / 1.5 L of the chicken stock, the pork and its fat, and the kielbasa. The liquid should cover the solids; if necessary, add more broth. Bring the soup to a simmer, add the bay leaves, then reduce the heat to low to maintain a gentle simmer. Cover the pot, leaving the lid slightly ajar, and simmer for 2 hours or until the pork is tender and the flavors are bright and acidic. Add the dried fruit and drained sauerkraut and simmer with the lid slightly ajar for 30 minutes more.

Taste the soup and add more salt or pepper if desired. Serve the soup hot, garnishing each serving with a dollop of sour cream, scallion rings, and dill. It will keep in the refrigerator for up to a week or in the freezer for up to 3 months.

APPLE KRAUT
MAKES ABOUT 2½ QUARTS / 2.5 L

The addition of a single tart apple to the cabbage as it ferments makes this zesty sauerkraut distinctive. If you have a mandoline, use it to slice the cabbage and apple very thinly; or shred them very finely with a knife.

- 1 large (3-pound / 1.4 kg) head green cabbage, halved, cored, and very thinly sliced
- 1 Granny Smith apple, peeled, cored, and very thinly sliced
- 3 tablespoons / 27 g kosher salt
- 1 tablespoon caraway seed

Sterilize a 3-quart / 3 L canning jar or fermentation crock. Combine the cabbage, apple, caraway, and salt in a very large bowl and massage gently for a few minutes to release some liquid. Press a heavy plate onto the cabbage and apple mix to weigh it down. Leave to stand at room temperature, tossing and squeezing the cabbage 4 or 5 more times, until it has released enough liquid to cover the solids, about 4 hours.

Pack the cabbage and its liquid into the sterilized jar or crock, using a spoon to completely submerge the cabbage in the liquid (if necessary, add a bit of salted water to cover). Seal the container, using a lid with an airlock if you have one; if you don't, open the container every few days to release carbon dioxide buildup and check for mold, which can gently be scraped off the ferment. Store at cool room temperature (ideally 60°F to 70°F / 15°C to 21°C) for at least 2 weeks, until the sauerkraut has a nice tang but is still crisp. Transfer the sauerkraut to the refrigerator, where it will keep for 12 months or more.

SAUERKRAUT POWDER
MAKES ABOUT ½ CUP / 65 G SAUERKRAUT POWDER

Sauerkraut powder is an excellent salt substitute that also adds appealing acidity. Try it as a garnish for just about any savory dish.

3 packed cups / 550 g drained sauerkraut

Spread the sauerkraut directly on the tray of a dehydrator and dehydrate the sauerkraut at 120°F / 48°C for 36 to 48 hours, stirring every 12 hours, until it crumbles easily between your fingers. This can also be done on a baking sheet in an oven with just the pilot light on or at 175°F / 80°C. Store in an airtight container in a cool, dry place for up to 6 months. Just before using, process the amount you need into a fine powder, using a spice grinder or mortar.

MAKES ABOUT 1 QUART *or* 1 LITER; SERVES 4 *to* 6

Carrot and Barberry Salad

This recipe was inspired by the Korean-Uzbek carrot salad that Russians fondly call morkovcha. But the salad actually stems from oppression. Beginning in 1860 and continuing into the early twentieth century, Koreans from the northeastern province of Hamkyŏng migrated to the Russian Far East in search of a better life. They established vibrant communities, which were uprooted in 1937 when Stalin forcibly deported nearly 200,000 Koreans to Uzbekistan, then part of the Soviet Union. Once again, the Koreans had to adapt to a new, harsh climate; in this case, a desert. Seaweed was no longer available, so the Koryo-saram, as they are known, began making a banchan-like carrot salad instead.

With the easing of restrictions after Stalin's death, some Koryo-saram moved to European parts of the USSR to work or to study. Their carrot salad followed, becoming a sought-after offering in the farmers' markets of Moscow and Leningrad. Spicy Korean salad soon became a ubiquitous dish on the Russian zakuska or appetizer table. It remains so popular that houseware stores sell special graters to make the fine julienne strips that define the salad's appealing texture.

Our recipe departs from the original, ramping up the salad's verve by including pickled carrots and barberries and heightening the Korean profile by adding gochujang, gochugaru, sesame oil, and sesame seeds. The finishing shower of cilantro adds a characteristic taste of Uzbekistan.

The pickled carrots and barberries keep for months in the refrigerator, so it's a good idea to make them well in advance. And if you like your salads especially zingy, feel free to add more dressing.

---

6 ounces / 170 g fresh carrots, peeled and cut into fine julienne strips
4 ounces / 115 g (2 small bunches) scallions, white and green parts, thinly sliced
4 ounces / 115 g (about 1 cup) drained Pickled Carrots (recipe follows)
¼ cup / 36 g drained Pickled Barberries (recipe follows)
¾ cup / 180 ml Spicy Sesame Dressing (recipe follows)
Toasted sesame seeds, for garnish
½ bunch coarsely chopped cilantro, for garnish

In a large bowl, combine the julienned fresh carrots, sliced scallions, and the pickled carrots. Stir in the pickled barberries.

Pour the dressing over the vegetables and toss until well coated. Leave the salad to marinate for at least 30 minutes at room temperature before serving. Leftovers will keep in the refrigerator for several days. To serve, garnish with toasted sesame seeds and chopped cilantro.

PICKLED CARROTS
MAKES ABOUT 1 QUART / 1 L

½ pound / 225 g carrots, peeled and cut into fine julienne strips
1 teaspoon toasted cumin seed
2 cups / 475 ml apple cider vinegar
1 cup / 240 ml water
7 tablespoons / 90 g granulated sugar
4½ tablespoons / 40 g kosher salt

Pack the julienned carrots and cumin seed into a sterilized 1-quart / 1 L canning jar. Bring the vinegar, water, sugar, and salt to a boil in a medium saucepan, stirring to dissolve the sugar and salt. Carefully pour the hot liquid over the carrots to cover them completely—the liquid can come all the way to the mouth of the jar. Leave to cool to room temperature, then cover the jar and refrigerate overnight before using. The carrots can be stored in the refrigerator for up to 2 months.

PICKLED BARBERRIES
MAKES ABOUT 2 CUPS / 480 ML

1 cup / 240 ml apple cider vinegar
¼ cup / 60 ml water
1 teaspoon kosher salt
½ cup / 32 g dried barberries
Freshly ground black pepper

Sterilize a 1-pint / 500 ml canning jar. Combine all the ingredients in a small saucepan over medium heat. Bring to a simmer and cook for 1 minute, then remove the pan from the heat and leave the mixture to cool. Transfer the berries and their brine to the jar and cover tightly with the lid. The barberries can be stored in the refrigerator for up to 2 months.

SPICY SESAME DRESSING
MAKES ABOUT 1¼ CUPS / 300 ML

6 garlic cloves, finely grated or minced
1 (1-inch / 2.5 cm) knob fresh ginger, peeled and finely grated
6 tablespoons / 90 ml light olive oil
3 tablespoons / 45 ml toasted sesame oil
6 tablespoons / 90 ml soy sauce
3 tablespoon / 45 ml rice vinegar
3 packed tablespoons / 41 g light brown sugar
1 tablespoon kosher salt
1 tablespoon cumin seed, toasted and coarsely ground
2 tablespoons gochugaru (Korean red chile flakes)
3 tablespoons toasted sesame seeds
2 tablespoons gochujang (Korean red chile paste)

In a small bowl, combine the garlic, ginger, olive oil, sesame oil, soy sauce, rice vinegar, brown sugar, salt, cumin, gochugaru, sesame seeds, and gochujang. Use immediately or store extra dressing in the refrigerator, where it will keep for 1 week.

MAKES ABOUT 1½ CUPS *or* 300 GRAMS

Charred Baba Ghanoush

If hummus has a rival in the Middle East, it's the eggplant dip baba ghanoush, which is eaten throughout the region. Its components vary from country to country, but the one constant is the wonderfully smoky flavor that results from charring the eggplant before scooping out its ultrasoft flesh.

The dip's charming name—"pampered papa" in Arabic—has inevitably led to conjectures about its origin. Was the papa in question a sultan whose harem spoiled him with this succulent dish, or a toothless old man whose devoted daughter served him soft food? We like to think of this papa as the pot-bellied eggplant itself, the pampered star of its own show.

Serve baba ghanoush with bread, as a dip or a spread, or offer it plain as an accompaniment to roast meat, especially lamb.

---

1 cup / 227 g Fermented Eggplant (recipe follows)
1 small garlic clove, minced
2 tablespoons / 35 g tahini
1½ tablespoons freshly squeezed lemon juice, or more to taste
¼ teaspoon ground cumin
A pinch of sumac powder
⅛ teaspoon smoked paprika
Salt and freshly ground black pepper, to taste
3 tablespoons / 45 ml extra-virgin olive oil
Chopped fresh parsley, for garnish
Olive or sesame oil, for garnish
Toasted sesame seeds, for garnish

In a medium bowl, stir together the fermented eggplant with the garlic, tahini, lemon juice, cumin, sumac, and paprika, and season with salt and pepper. Drizzle in the olive oil while slowly whisking with a fork until you have a silky emulsion.

Taste for seasoning, adding more salt, pepper, or lemon juice, if desired. Transfer the baba ghanoush to a serving dish. Garnish with chopped parsley, a drizzle of olive or sesame oil, and toasted sesame seeds. The baba ghanoush will keep for up to a week in the refrigerator.

MAKES ABOUT 4 CUPS *or* 500 GRAMS

Fermented Eggplant

The secret to a successful purée is to make sure that the eggplants are baked all the way through, until they are soft enough to collapse. It also helps to seek out young eggplants that don't feel heavy when you pick them up, since they're likely to have fewer seeds. This purée thickens as it ferments, so don't be surprised when you open the jar to find that it has solidified.

3 pounds / 1.4 kg medium globe eggplants
8 large garlic cloves, peeled and minced
Kosher salt
½ cup / 120 ml olive oil

Preheat a grill to high. Place the whole eggplants directly on the grates and char them on all sides until the skin is completely blackened and the flesh inside is soft to the touch. This should take 15 to 20 minutes. Alternatively, you can char them over an open flame on a gas stove or broil them in the oven. If the eggplants are large and the flesh hasn't thoroughly softened once they have charred, transfer them to a hot oven and cook until they're fully tender inside.

Transfer the eggplants to a bowl, cover with a towel, and leave them to cool. Once they are cool enough to handle, use a sharp paring knife to carefully slit each eggplant lengthwise. Scoop the soft flesh out of the charred skin with a large spoon; discard the skin.

Transfer the flesh to a fine-mesh strainer set over a large bowl. Pick out and discard any stray bits of skin or blackened flesh that may have mixed in during the scooping process. Place a small plate on top of the eggplant to weight it down slightly, and leave the eggplant to drain for about 2 hours, until it has released all excess moisture. Discard the liquid.

Place the empty bowl on a kitchen scale and tare to subtract the weight of the bowl, then add the drained eggplant flesh and the garlic to the bowl. Calculate 2 percent of the combined weight of the eggplant and garlic, and measure out that weight of kosher salt. Transfer the eggplant and garlic to a food processor and add the salt. Process into a smooth, creamy purée.

Sterilize a 1-quart / 1 L glass or ceramic container with a lid. Transfer the purée to the container, and wipe off any bits of eggplant that stick to the rim or sides. Place a piece of plastic wrap directly atop the surface of the purée and seal the container with its lid. Leave the mixture to ferment at room temperature (60°F to 68°F / 15°C to 20°C) for 1 week, periodically checking for mold, which can be scraped off the ferment. At this point, the saltiness will have faded into the background, leaving the purée with a tangy flavor. Remove the lid and the plastic wrap, pour the oil over the surface of the purée to cover it, and seal it and replace the lid (discard the plastic). Store in the refrigerator, where it will keep for up to 1 year.

MAKES ABOUT 2 QUARTS *or* 2 LITERS

Eggplant Makdous

These miniature eggplants bursting with walnuts, garlic, and red peppers are just one of the treasures of Arabic preserves. The name makdous *comes from the practice of layering the eggplants into jars for storage. Eggplant makdous is prepared throughout the Middle East, though it is most closely associated with Syria and Lebanon. Making these preserves has traditionally been a collective activity among women and children, who begin to stuff eggplants as soon as they ripen, in late September or October.*

It's important to choose small eggplants for stuffing. Not only are they visually more appealing in this preparation, they have fewer seeds and are less bitter. The original method of preserving in oil has not changed for centuries; because the thick layer of oil keeps air from penetrating the eggplants, they will keep for a good year, absorbing flavor from both the oil and their savory filling. The longer they sit, the tastier they become, developing an appealing sourness.

Serve these eggplants as part of a mezze spread or on a charcuterie board, or stuff a few into pita for a delicious lunch.

1½ pounds / 680 g small (3-inch / 7.5 cm) eggplants, such as Indian eggplants
About 2 quarts / 2 L olive oil
Kosher salt

FILLING
1 medium sweet red pepper
1 small hot pepper, such as cayenne or bird's eye (optional)
1 teaspoon salt
1½ cups / 180 g walnuts, toasted and chopped or coarsely crushed
4 garlic cloves, finely minced
½ teaspoon ground cumin
½ teaspoon ground paprika
¼ teaspoon ground coriander
⅛ teaspoon ground cinnamon
Additional salt and freshly ground black pepper, to taste

Thoroughly wash the eggplants and remove the stems. Slit each eggplant lengthwise halfway through the flesh.

In a medium sauté pan over medium heat, heat enough olive oil to cover the bottom of the pan by ⅛ to ¼ inch / 3 to 6 mm. Sear the eggplants in batches, turning them frequently, until they are slightly tender and the skins begin to blister and brown, 8 to 10 minutes. If they are browning too much before they have turned tender, lower the heat. Alternatively, place them on a baking sheet in a 300°F / 150°C oven and bake for 3 to 8 minutes, depending on the size of the eggplants. Whichever method you use, the eggplants are done when the tip of a knife penetrates the flesh easily, yet they remain firm enough to stuff.

Transfer the eggplants to a perforated pan set over a larger roasting pan, leaving a little space between each one. When the eggplants are cool enough to handle, apply a small amount of salt to their insides. Place another roasting pan, baking sheet, or plate on top of the eggplants to weigh them down; top this with a heavy weight, such as a couple of bricks or food cans, or even a large book. CONTINUED ▸

EGGPLANT MAKDOUS CONTINUED

This salting and pressing is crucial in order to extract as much moisture as possible. Leave the eggplants under pressure for up to 24 hours at room temperature. Check them periodically, discarding the water from the bottom pan when you do; if you notice a significant amount of water pooling around the eggplants or at the bottom of the container, they are still releasing moisture, so continue to press them. The eggplants are ready to stuff when they have become slightly flattened and compressed and feel firmer and denser than they were at the start—they should not be left long enough to turn soft or mushy.

Once the eggplants are ready, sterilize two 1-quart/1 L wide-mouth canning jars. Then prepare the filling. Remove the stems and seeds from both the sweet and hot peppers and chop the peppers into chunks, then pulse them with the 1 teaspoon of salt in a food processor until they are finely chopped but not puréed. Transfer them to a fine-mesh sieve placed over a bowl to drain for at least 15 minutes. Press down on the peppers to release all of their juice, which you can discard or reserve for another use.

Turn the drained peppers into a bowl and add the walnuts, garlic, cumin, paprika, coriander, and cinnamon. Season to taste with salt and pepper. Generously stuff each eggplant with this filling until each one is brimming. Squeeze the eggplants gently to enclose the filling so that it doesn't fall out during the curing process.

Layer the stuffed eggplants into the jars, seasoning each layer with a little salt. Leave about 1 inch/2.5 cm of headroom at the top. Pour enough olive oil into the jars to cover the eggplants—you will need about 3 cups/720 ml for each jar. Let the oil settle, then top with a little more to make sure the eggplants are completely covered. Seal the jars airtight.

Leave the eggplants to cure for 2 weeks at room temperature (68°F to 72°F/20°C to 22°C). They will keep at room temperature for about 1 year as long as the eggplants are fully submerged; whenever you remove some, top off the oil as necessary.

MAKES 1 QUART *or* 1 LITER

Ajvar

This concentrated red pepper spread is beloved throughout the Balkans, where it is found in many different iterations. Serbians like it unadorned to feature the four basic ingredients: red peppers, oil, vinegar, and salt. Macedonians typically add eggplant and sometimes sugar. Some people prefer their ajvar smooth, while others like it slightly chunky. It can be mild, or made spicy with the addition of hot peppers.

Cultural battles rage as to the spread's provenance, but no one disputes that the name ajvar *(pronounced EYE-var) comes from the Turkish word for caviar. The Ottomans introduced New World peppers and sunflowers in the sixteenth century, and the comparison to caviar likely arose because peppers and sunflower oil were expensive ingredients. Today, when the ingredients are common and inexpensive, ajvar is considered a necessity instead of a luxury. It provides vitamins to help sustain people through the region's cold winters, while offering a welcome brightness and piquancy.*

Our version of ajvar is spicy, but feel free to use fewer hot peppers—just be sure that you start with a total quantity of 3 pounds/1.4 kg of peppers, whether mild or hot. (You can always halve the recipe, keeping the proportions the same.) And don't bypass the first step of charring the peppers, as the roasted flavor is essential. Serve ajvar with bread, as part of a cheese and charcuterie platter, or as a lively accompaniment to meat, especially sausage.

2½ pounds/1.1 kg long sweet or mild red peppers, such as Marconi or red Cubanelle

8 ounces/225 g hot red peppers, such as cayenne or red jalapeño

1 pound/454 g eggplant, pricked all over with a fork

8 garlic cloves, minced

⅓ cup/80 ml olive oil, plus more for storage

2 tablespoons sherry vinegar or red wine vinegar

1 tablespoon kosher salt

2 teaspoons smoked paprika

½ teaspoon freshly ground black pepper

½ teaspoon ground cumin

1 teaspoon ground coriander

Preheat a grill to high heat, or turn a stovetop gas burner to high. Working in batches, if necessary, place the whole peppers and eggplant directly on the grill or over the burner flame. Roast the vegetables, turning them occasionally with tongs, until the skins are charred and blistered all over. The peppers will take about 10 minutes, and the eggplant up to 30 minutes, to char and soften completely inside.

Once they are roasted, immediately transfer the peppers to a bowl and cover it with plastic wrap or a clean kitchen towel. Set aside for 15 minutes or more to steam the peppers and make it easier to peel off the charred skin. Transfer the eggplant to another bowl or plate to cool. When the peppers are cool enough to handle, gently peel off the charred skin with your fingers; it should come off easily. Don't fret if some charred flecks of skin remain, and do not rinse the peppers under water, as that will remove some of the delicious charred flavor. Slice off the tops of the peppers, remove the seeds and membranes, and place the peppers in the bowl of a food processor or the jar of a blender. Slit the eggplant lengthwise and scoop out the flesh. Add this to the peppers. CONTINUED ▶

VEGETABLES

AJVAR CONTINUED

Add the minced garlic, olive oil, vinegar, salt, and spices to the peppers and eggplant. Pulse or blend until the mixture reaches the consistency you like. Transfer the ajvar to a heavy-bottom pot and cook over medium heat, stirring frequently, for 30 minutes to concentrate it slightly. Taste and adjust the seasoning, adding a little more salt, pepper, or vinegar if necessary.

Since the flavors develop as the ajvar sits, it tastes best when left, covered, at room temperature for a few hours or overnight. Transfer the ajvar to a sterilized, airtight 1-quart / 1 L jar and top with enough olive oil to completely cover the spread. Seal the jar tightly with a lid and refrigerate. The ajvar will last for 3 months. For longer storage, process the jar of spread in a hot water bath according to the manufacturer's instructions.

THE BLUE GODDESS

Fermentation works its magic well beyond the realm of the kitchen. The color indigo derives from the green leaves of the *Indigofera tinctoria* plant, which bacteria transform into a rich, deep shade of violet-blue. Dyers in South India, who perfected this rather amazing process thousands of years ago, to this day refer to the dye as the "blue goddess." To make indigo, *Indigofera* leaves are left to ferment in a large vat of water before being exposed to air, which turns them a vivid blue. They then undergo a second fermentation with an alkaline additive, during which the liquid reverts to a dull greenish-brown. When fabric is dipped into the vat and exposed to air the blue reappears, this time as the fabric's dye.

Due to the laborious production method, indigo has historically commanded high prices. Only elites could afford fabric dyed with true indigo, which became a prized commodity for the British in India, as well as in colonial South Carolina, where this "blue gold" supported the cash economy. Enslaved people carried out the onerous labor of producing the dye, which was sent to England's textile mills. After the British lost the American colonies, they turned increased attention to India, where officers of the British Raj eventually forced farmers to grow indigo in place of the food crops they desperately needed. Meanwhile, commoners in England had long been extracting blue dye from a plant called woad (*Isatis tinctoria*). Woad dye wasn't as colorfast as true indigo and was therefore less prized. Therefore, English dyers campaigned to limit imports of true indigo from India, referring to Indian indigo as "the devil's dye" to underscore its pernicious means of production. Nevertheless, the indigo import trade remained lucrative until the late nineteenth century, when German chemists succeeded in creating a much less expensive synthetic blue dye.

In the US, workers wore indigo-dyed shirt collars, rather than white ones that more readily revealed the dirt, thus giving rise to the term "blue-collar workers." Levi's blue jeans, which used natural indigo dye when they first came on the market in 1873, famously became part of the working man's uniform, though after their embrace by celebrities in the late twentieth century, they entered the realm of fashion. Although most Levi's are now dyed with synthetic color, the company has within the past decade introduced natural indigo dyes for certain product lines, promoting its uniquely beautiful color.

And its loveliness is incomparable: when Sir Isaac Newton, in his theory of the visible spectrum, introduced indigo as one of the seven colors of the rainbow, he had noted its special properties, calling it "visible yet immaterial, the color purest in meaning, with the power to negotiate the two spheres of God and man."

MAKES ABOUT 2 QUARTS *or* 2 LITERS

Zesty Asparagus Pickles

We were so smitten with the irresistible zing of our asparagus pickles that we almost named them after beloved bread-and-butter pickles, that staple of American cookouts and lunchboxes. Bread-and-butter pickles have appealing lore, such as the claim that these everyday pickles, served between slices of buttered bread, were a Depression-era staple; or the fact that the name had been trademarked in the 1920s by an Illinois cucumber farmer and his wife, who supposedly bartered their homemade pickles for bread and butter at the local store. The truth is that classic bread-and-butter pickles rely heavily on sugar—standard recipes contain nearly twice as much sugar as vinegar—and our pickles flip that script. So we gave up on the name, even though these habit-forming pickles have become nearly as standard in our kitchens as bread and butter.

2 pounds / 900 g asparagus spears
2 cups / 480 ml white wine vinegar
½ cup / 120 ml apple cider vinegar
1¼ cups / 300 ml water
½ cup / 100 g granulated sugar
5 tablespoons / 45 g kosher salt
1 teaspoon yellow mustard seed
1 teaspoon celery seed
1 teaspoon powdered turmeric
1 teaspoon red pepper flakes, or more to taste
4 garlic cloves, peeled and smashed
4 or 5 large shallots, peeled and sliced thinly into rings

Sterilize two 1-quart / 1 L canning jars. Trim the asparagus spears by snapping them above the woody ends. Trim them to fit into the jars, saving the bottoms for another use.

Prepare an ice-water bath by filling a large bowl halfway with ice water and ice cubes. Bring a large pot of water to a boil, then add the asparagus spears and blanch them for 1 to 2 minutes, until they turn a vibrant green. Immediately transfer the asparagus to the ice-water bath to halt the cooking process, then drain and set aside.

In a medium pot, combine the white wine vinegar, apple cider vinegar, water, sugar, salt, mustard seed, celery seed, turmeric, red pepper, and garlic. Bring to a boil and simmer for about 5 minutes. Remove the pot from the heat and cool the brine to room temperature.

Pack the blanched asparagus and the shallots into the sterilized jars, leaving enough space at the top for the pickling brine to cover. Carefully pour the cooled brine over the asparagus and shallots, making sure to cover them completely. Seal the jars with their lids and refrigerate for at least 24 hours before serving to allow the flavors to meld. This pickle will keep in the refrigerator for at least 6 months.

MAKES 1 QUART *or* 1 LITER

Cucumbers Brined in a Pumpkin

A taste for the sour is embedded in the DNA of Russia, one of the world's great fermentation cultures. Some sort of salt-brined pickle appears at nearly every meal, as do sourdough black bread and smetana, aka cultured cream, all washed down with kvass or vodka—both also products of fermentation. In summertime, Russians ferment fruit—especially watermelon and berries—in addition to vegetables, but the real work begins after the fall harvest, when hundreds of pounds of cucumbers and cabbages are turned into pickles and sauerkraut to carry people through the long, hard winter. Privation is the mother of inventive flavors, as well as of preserving.

One old method for making pickles calls for fermenting them inside a pumpkin, which lends the pickles a subtle flavor. The filled pumpkin was traditionally placed in a barrel with more cucumbers and brine distributed around it. To guarantee crisp pickles, Elena Molokhovets, the author of Russia's most famous nineteenth-century cookbook, recommends making a decoction of oak bark to add to the barrel brine. Lacking a legion of serfs to carry out this laborious step, we approximate her advice by suggesting you add fresh horseradish, cherry, or black currant leaves, though this is not crucial to the recipe's success. If you can't find these tannic aromatics, you can drop in some oak leaves—just be sure to wash them well first.

Never at a loss for advice to give, Molokhovets offers an additional step to ensure that the pickles remain crisp: salt your cucumbers 5 or 6 days after the full moon and finish the salting before the next new moon rises. Even if you choose not to attune your curing to the phases of the moon, the fermentation time depends on how sour you like your pickles. Deli-style half-sours will generally be ready in 3 days, while fully soured pickles can take up to 5 days.

As a bonus if you've used a pumpkin that's good for baking, once you've finished using the pumpkin for pickling, you can cut it in half and bake it at 350°F/180°C until it's tender. Purée the baked pumpkin and stir in some butter and maple syrup to make a side dish. Waste not, want not.

---

2 to 3 pounds / .9 to 1.4 kg pickling cucumbers, preferably small (3-inch / 7.5 cm) Kirbys

2 quarts / 2 L water for the brine, plus additional ice water for soaking

1 (6-pound / 2.7 kg) pumpkin, preferably sugar or Cinderella

½ cup / 72 g kosher salt

1 to 1½ cups / 30 to 45 g assorted herbs (such as parsley, dill, celery leaves, and tarragon), and tannic leaves (such as horseradish, cherry, black currant, or oak)

8 large garlic cloves, peeled and lightly smashed

1 or 2 hot peppers, such as bird's eye or cayenne, stemmed and halved lengthwise

2 bay leaves

1 teaspoon allspice berries

1 teaspoon black peppercorns

Rinse the cucumbers well and slice off the blossom ends. Soak them in a large bowl of ice water for a few hours—this helps them maintain their crispness.

While the cucumbers are soaking, wash the pumpkin and cut out a lid from the top, as though you were making a jack-o'-lantern. Remove the seeds and scrape the flesh clean.

CONTINUED ▶

CUCUMBERS BRINED IN A PUMPKIN CONTINUED

Drain the cucumbers. In a large bowl, mix the 2 quarts/2 L water with the salt to make a 3.5 percent brine, stirring until the salt dissolves.

Place a layer of cucumbers in the bottom of the pumpkin, add a handful of herbs along with some of the garlic and hot peppers, then sprinkle in some of the spices (the bay, allspice, and peppercorns). Continue to layer the cucumbers and seasonings, saving a layer of tannic leaves for the top. Pour in the brine, which should completely cover the ingredients; if it doesn't, make more. Add the tannic leaves and cover the pumpkin with its lid, aligning it to close tightly.

Leave the cucumbers to ferment at room temperature (68°F to 72°F/20°C to 22°C) for 2 to 5 days, tasting them daily after 2 days have elapsed, until they have soured to your liking. Serve the pickles directly from the pumpkin. For longer storage, transfer them along with their brine to a jar and store in the refrigerator.

MAKES ABOUT 7 CUPS *or* 1.7 LITERS

Pickled Gazpacho with Charred Tomatoes and Peppers

Our version of gazpacho, Spain's cold summer soup, gets a lift from several fermented and cured ingredients: salt-brined cucumbers (page 34), preserved lemon, anchovies, and miso, all of which add exciting dimensions to the soup's standard profile. Charring the tomatoes and peppers also elevates the flavor, though that step is skippable for those in a hurry. A loaf of crusty bread is all that's needed to round out a meal.

2½ pounds / 1.1 kg tomatoes
3 sweet red peppers, such as Corno di Toro, piquillo, or bell
10 ounces / 280 g Cucumbers Brined in a Pumpkin (page 34), chopped
½ cup / 30 g lightly packed chopped parsley leaves
2 tablespoons lightly packed chopped cilantro leaves
2 tablespoons lightly packed chopped dill leaves
2 tablespoons lightly packed basil leaves
¼ preserved lemon, seeded and diced
1 large shallot, minced
3 anchovy fillets, minced
2 garlic cloves, minced or grated on a microplane
½ serrano chile, minced or grated on a microplane
2 tablespoons sherry vinegar
1 tablespoon kosher salt
1 teaspoon coriander seed, toasted and ground
1 teaspoon cumin seed, toasted and ground
1 teaspoon smoked paprika
1 teaspoon freshly ground black pepper
½ cup / 120 ml brine from salt-brined cucumbers (page 34)
1 tablespoon white miso
5 tablespoons / 75 ml extra-virgin olive oil

To char the tomatoes and peppers, set a metal grate directly over a gas burner, heat a grill to medium-high, or preheat an oven broiler. Arrange the tomatoes on the grate or grill over the flame, or on a pan under the broiler. After a minute or two, the skins will blister. Carefully turn the tomatoes to blister the other side, then transfer them to a plate. Char the peppers in a similar manner, giving them a little more time than the tomatoes to blacken their skins deeply. Place the charred peppers in a paper bag or in a bowl covered with plastic wrap to help the skins release.

When the tomatoes are cool enough to handle, peel away as much of the skin as you can, remove their cores, and cut them into chunks. Place in a large bowl. As soon as the peppers have cooled, carefully peel off the skins, remove the stems, scrape out the seeds, and dice the peppers. Transfer them to the bowl with the tomatoes. Stir in the remaining ingredients, except for the pickle brine, miso, and olive oil.

Working in batches, gently pulse the mixture in the bowl of a food processor until all of the vegetables and herbs are well combined. Don't over-process them: you want the finished soup to have a rustic consistency. Pour the mixture into a large, sealable container.

Ladle about 2 cups / 480 ml of the mixture into a blender. Add the pickle brine and miso and purée until very smooth. With the blender still running, stream in the olive oil. Scrape the purée into the container with the soup mixture and stir well to combine. Seal the container and refrigerate the soup for at least 1 hour, until thoroughly chilled, then taste for seasoning before serving. It will keep for 3 days.

MAKES ABOUT 1 QUART *or* 1 LITER

Tangy Corn on the Cob

Few vegetables present as many options for preserving and creative reinterpretation as corn. Its kernels, husks, and cobs become templates for inventive dishes around the globe, from the nixtamalization process that begets the masa used in tortillas, posole, and tamales in Mexico and Central America, to the coarse maize powder that Indian cooks mix with spices to prepare makki ki roti. The Appalachian technique of fermenting sweet corn during its relatively short season, imparting a pleasantly sour tang to the kernels, is another example. For this recipe, we keep the kernels on the cobs, submerging them in a salt brine with fresh chile, ginger, shallots, and spices, which balance the tang of fermentation with depth and heat. The resulting corn, ready in as little as a week, can be eaten off the cob as is, lightly grilled with butter and herbs, or scraped off the cob and turned into a delicious corn relish (page 42).

3 ears corn
4 garlic cloves, thinly sliced
1 chile pepper, such as serrano or red jalapeño, stemmed and thinly sliced
2 shallots, thinly sliced
1 teaspoon coriander seed, toasted
1 teaspoon fennel seed, toasted
1 teaspoon whole black peppercorns
Water
Kosher salt

Sterilize both a wide-mouth 2-quart /2 L canning jar and a fermentation weight or small dish that will fit inside the jar to keep the cobs submerged in the brine. Shuck the corn, setting aside the silk to add to the ferment. Cut each ear straight through the cob into 3 or 4 pieces. Place the corn silk, garlic, chile, shallots, coriander, fennel, and black pepper in the jar, add the corn pieces, and pour in enough water to completely cover them. As you do, keep track of how much water you add, since this will dictate the amount of salt you need, which is 3 percent salt based on the weight of the water (see Salt, page 99).

Measure out the salt and add it to the jar; stir with a long wooden spoon, then screw the lid on the jar and shake it well until the salt is dissolved. Remove the lid and place the sterilized weight on top of the corn to keep the cobs submerged in the brine. Seal the container, using a lid with an airlock if you have one; if you don't, open the container every few days to release carbon dioxide buildup and check for mold, which can be gently lifted off the ferment. Place the container in a clean, low-light area with an ambient temperature of 62°F to 68°F/17°C to 20°C until the corn tastes nicely sour, 1 to 2 weeks.

MAKES ABOUT 6 CUPS *or* 1.5 LITERS

Warm Corn Relish

This summery combo of corn, beans, and squash can be used as a relish or served as a side salad. It's partly inspired by the Native American practice of planting corn, beans, and squash in symbiotic proximity, a combination that the Iroquois dubbed the "Three Sisters." The relish also recalls the Cajun dish maque choux, the spicy Louisiana cousin of succotash. We make our version even more beguiling by grilling sweet corn and then adding a little sour corn that we've fermented on the cob. Scraping the kernels from the cobs and then "milking" the cobs with a knife ensures that the finished dish will be creamy.

3 ears fresh corn
1 ear (3 chunks) Tangy Corn on the Cob (page 41)
6 tablespoons / 90 ml light olive oil
4 ounces / 115 g shallots, halved and sliced thinly into half moons (about 1 cup)
2 teaspoons kosher salt
¼ cup / 28 g small-diced celery rib
½ cup / 60 g small-diced red bell pepper
4 ounces / 115 g green beans, cut into ¼-inch / 6 mm rounds (about 1 cup)
6 ounces / 170 g summer squash, cut into medium dice
2 garlic cloves, minced
½ to 1 jalapeño or serrano chile, minced (or more for extra kick)
½ teaspoon chopped fresh marjoram or oregano leaves
½ teaspoon chopped fresh thyme leaves
⅛ teaspoon smoked paprika
⅛ teaspoon ground coriander
⅛ teaspoon ground cumin
⅛ teaspoon freshly ground black pepper
¼ cup / 60 ml corn brine (from Tangy Corn on the Cob, page 41)
Salt and pepper, to taste
¼ cup / 35 g toasted pumpkin seeds
¼ cup / 4 g roughly chopped parsley leaves

Peel back most of the corn husks, leaving only a couple of layers to protect the corn ears while grilling, and trim the silk from the tips of the ears. Preheat a grill to medium (350°F to 400°F / 180°C to 200°C). Place the corn over direct heat and grill for 20 to 25 minutes, turning frequently, until even grill marks and a nice sear appear all over the husks. Remove the grilled corn from the heat and leave it to cool.

Remove the remaining husks and any remaining corn silk, then cut the kernels from the cob and transfer them to a bowl. Placing each scraped cob in the bowl, apply pressure to them with the blunt side of a knife, swiping up and down to extract any remaining corn milk. (The cobs and silk can be reserved for making Sweet Corn Tea, page 47.) Using the same method, remove the kernels from the Tangy Corn and add it to the bowl with the grilled corn.

Gently heat the olive oil in a medium sauté pan over medium heat. Add the shallots and salt and cook, stirring frequently, for 3 to 5 minutes, until they begin to soften. Add the bell peppers, celery, and green beans and stir to combine. Cook for another 5 minutes, then add the diced summer squash. Continue to stir and cook for an additional 3 minutes. CONTINUED ▶

WARM CORN RELISH CONTINUED

Stir in the minced garlic, jalapeño, fresh herbs, and dried spices. Cook, stirring frequently, for 3 to 5 minutes more, until the mixture is fragrant. Add the corn brine to the pan, turn the heat to high, and allow the relish to simmer for a few minutes until slightly reduced. Then add all of the corn kernels, both grilled and tangy, to the pan. Stir to combine, cover the pan, and cook for just 2 minutes to warm the relish. Remove the pan from the heat and taste for seasoning, adding more salt and pepper if desired. Just before serving, stir in the toasted pumpkin seeds and the parsley.

Serve warm or at room temperature.

MAKES ABOUT 7 CUPS *or* 1.7 LITERS

Sweet Corn Tea

In summer, when corn is at its sweetest, strip off the kernels for your favorite corn recipe but retain the cobs and silk, which become the base for sweet corn cob tea. Corn silk tea and variations that include the cobs have purported health benefits from improving digestion to strengthening gums. For this version, we focus foremost on flavor, creating a concentrated reduction with corn cobs and silk, blueberries, lemony herbs, vanilla, and cardamom, then adding honey and lemon juice before blending it with brewed black tea. After refrigerating the mixture, we serve it over ice for a refreshing, pleasantly sweet, and memorable drink.

4 ears fresh corn
10 cups / 2.4 L water
1 cup / 240 ml freshly squeezed lemon juice (from approximately 6 lemons), plus 3 of the lemons' rinds, reserved after juicing
1 cup / 150 g blueberries
6 sprigs lemon balm or lemon verbena
½ vanilla bean, split lengthwise but not scraped
2 cardamom pods, lightly smashed
6 to 8 tablespoons / 125 to 165 g raw honey, to taste
8 black tea bags

Shuck the corn. Remove the silk and set it aside. Carefully cut the kernels off the cobs and set aside for another use, such as Warm Corn Relish (page 42).

In a narrow pot with high sides, bring 6 cups / 1.5 L of the water to a boil. Cut the corn cobs in halves or thirds and add the cobs, reserved corn silk, 3 lemon rinds, blueberries, 3 sprigs of lemon balm or verbena, ½ vanilla bean, and smashed cardamom pods to the boiling water. Reduce the heat, cover, and simmer the mixture for about 30 minutes, then strain the solids and discard them.

Return the strained liquid to the pot and simmer it over low heat until it reduces by half, to about 3 cups / 720 ml, which concentrates the corn flavor. Remove this reduction from the heat and stir in the lemon juice and honey.

In a separate pot, bring the remaining 4 cups / 1 L of the water to a boil and drop in the tea bags. Remove the pot from the heat, cover, and steep the tea bags for 12 to 15 minutes; remove the tea bags. In a pitcher or a large jar, combine the brewed tea with the corn reduction. Stir well, adding more honey to taste.

Refrigerate the tea for at least 2 hours, until it is well chilled. Serve over ice. Sweet Corn Tea will keep in the refrigerator for 3 to 4 weeks.

MAKES ABOUT 1 QUART *or* 1 LITER; SERVES 4 *to* 6 *as a* SIDE DISH

Vinegret

The mixed vegetable salad known in Russian as vinegret *originated in the eighteenth century, when French cooks imported by the aristocracy introduced the word* vinaigrette, *referring to a light dressing of vinegar and olive oil. But in Russia, the word* vinegret *more familiarly came to refer to a salad of mixed vegetables and then, by extension, to any grab bag of elements—even weather-related, as when describing mixed precipitation.*

The salad's components have never been fixed, although typically (this being Russia) vinegret includes beets, along with fermented or pickled vegetables to add sharpness. Once potatoes were widely planted, in the mid-nineteenth century, they too became a usual ingredient. Many recipes for vinegret also call for wild fowl or herring. The original oil and vinegar dressing was often enhanced with or replaced by a creamy concoction made with mayonnaise or sour cream.

During Soviet times, vinegret became a dietary mainstay—even during periods of food shortages, the ingredients remained available and affordable. So embedded was the salad in Russian life that when the Bolsheviks mandated name changes to rid dishes of any vestigial reference to their bourgeois origins, vinegret was spared.

In the spirit of a free-for-all salad, we've modernized vinegret to include not just shaved Brussels sprouts and sunflower seeds but also a trifecta of beets: roasted, pickled, and fermented. We marinate the vegetables briefly in a classic vinaigrette dressing before dousing them with a creamy, herb-filled sauce that faintly recalls ranch dressing. If your vegetables are a bit larger or smaller than indicated below—just keep the amounts roughly in balance. And although the salad isn't hard to make, it is time-consuming; we suggest making it in stages. Then you can quickly throw the salad together not long before serving. This version of vinegret tastes best the same day it is made.

---

1 medium (5 ounces / 140 g) red beet
Olive oil
Kosher salt
2 small potatoes (7 ounces / 200 g total)
1 medium (4½ ounces / 130 g) carrot
1½ ounces / 43 g fermented beets, ½-inch / 1.25 cm dice (¼ cup)
3 ounces / 85 g Pickled Beets (page 87), ½-inch / 1.25 cm dice (½ cup)
8 to 10 raw Brussels sprouts, finely shaved to yield 1 cup / 90 g
2¼ ounces / 65 g fermented cucumber, ¼-inch / 6 mm dice (scant ½ cup)
¼ cup / 13 g packed coarsely chopped dill fronds, plus more for garnish

¼ cup / 19 g packed coarsely chopped parsley leaves
½ ounce / 16 g scallions, white and green parts, ¼-inch / 6 mm rounds (¼ cup)
1 cup / 127 g Toasted Sunflower Seeds (page 50)
½ cup / 120 ml Shallot Vinaigrette (page 50)
Freshly ground pepper
¾ cup / 180 ml Creamy Dressing (page 51)
Finely grated fresh horseradish, for garnish

CONTINUED ▶

VINEGRET CONTINUED

Preheat the oven to 350°F/180°C. Place the beet in a small, ovenproof dish, add splashes of water and olive oil, and cover it tightly. Bake for about 1 hour, until it is easily pierced with a skewer. Set aside to cool, then peel the beet and dice it into ½-inch/1.25 cm cubes. You should have ¾ cup/135 g of diced beet.

While the beet is baking, prepare the potatoes and carrots by peeling them and dicing them into ½-inch/1.25 cm cubes. You should end up with 1 cup/175 g of potatoes and ½ cup/100 g of carrots.

Place the diced potatoes and carrots on two separate baking sheets, toss with olive oil and salt, and cover the pans with foil. Bake at 350°F / 180°C until they are still firm but easily pierced with a skewer, 20 to 25 minutes. Set aside to cool.

Once all the baked vegetables have cooled, place them in a large bowl and add the fermented and pickled beets along with the Brussels sprouts, fermented cucumber, dill, parsley, scallions, and sunflower seeds. Stream in the shallot vinaigrette and toss the ingredients together gently. Add salt and pepper to taste, then leave the salad to absorb the vinaigrette for 20 to 30 minutes at room temperature before adding the creamy dressing. Transfer to a serving bowl and garnish with dill and horseradish. You can toss on more sunflower seeds, if desired.

TOASTED SUNFLOWER SEEDS
MAKES ABOUT 2 CUPS / 254 G

1 teaspoon unsalted butter
1 tablespoon raw honey
Grated zest of 1 lemon
2 teaspoons kosher salt
1 ¾ cups /225 g sunflower seeds
1 teaspoon smoked hot paprika

Preheat the oven to 350°F/180°C. In a small saucepan over medium heat, melt the butter with the honey, lemon zest, and salt. Add the sunflower seeds and stir them to coat in the mixture, then spread the seeds in a single layer on a sheet pan. Bake until lightly toasted, about 12 minutes. Remove the seeds from the oven, toss with the paprika, and allow to cool. The seeds can be toasted up to 3 days in advance and stored in an airtight container at room temperature.

SHALLOT VINAIGRETTE
MAKES ABOUT 1 CUP / 240 ML

½ large shallot, finely minced (¼ cup/45 g)
5 tablespoons/75 ml freshly squeezed lemon juice
¾ teaspoon caraway seed
1 tablespoon apple cider vinegar
1 tablespoon Dijon mustard
1½ teaspoons raw honey
½ teaspoon fennel pollen, or ¼ teaspoon each toasted and ground fennel seed and aniseed
1 tablespoon/9 g kosher salt
Plenty of freshly cracked black pepper
6 tablespoons/90 ml light extra-virgin olive oil
3 tablespoons/45 ml cold-pressed sunflower oil

In a small bowl, macerate the shallot in the lemon juice for 10 to 15 minutes to mellow its sharpness. Meanwhile, toast the caraway seed in a dry pan over medium heat for a couple of minutes until fragrant, then grind the seeds in a spice grinder. You should end up with ½ teaspoon.

Add the caraway to the macerated shallot, along with the vinegar, mustard, honey, fennel pollen, salt, and pepper. Slowly whisk in the olive oil and sunflower oil until the vinaigrette is slightly emulsified. Taste and adjust the salt, pepper, and honey to your liking.

CREAMY DRESSING
MAKES 1 CUP / 240 ML

5 tablespoons/75 g sour cream
5 tablespoons/75 g mayonnaise
6 tablespoons/90 ml full-fat buttermilk
½ to 1 serrano chile, seeded and finely minced
1 teaspoon powdered garlic
1 teaspoon powdered onion
¼ cup/13 g finely minced chives
¼ cup/13 g finely minced dill
¼ cup/19 g finely minced parsley
2 teaspoons finely minced marjoram
2 teaspoons finely minced tarragon
1 tablespoon lemon juice
1 teaspoon kosher salt
½ teaspoon freshly ground black pepper

In a medium bowl, combine all the ingredients and mix until well combined. Transfer to an airtight container and refrigerate for up to 1 week.

MAKES 12 FRITTERS; SERVES 4

Vegetable Fritters

If you love latkes as much as we do, you'll be delighted to meet their root-vegetable cousins. Crisp on the outside and creamy within, these fritters require less oil for frying, yet they're equally moreish. You do need to plan ahead for this recipe, but if you keep a stash of fermented root vegetables in the fridge, you can whip up these fritters in no time. And you can play around with their flavor profile by using a different mix of vegetables whenever you make a new batch.

8 ounces/225 g Fermented Whole Vegetables (recipe follows)
6 ounces/170 g raw Japanese sweet potato, peeled (or substitute garnet yam)
4 ounces/115 g raw parsnip, peeled
½ cup/70 g white rice flour
½ cup finely grated Parmesan cheese
1 tablespoon kosher salt
1 teaspoon smoked paprika
1 teaspoon caraway seed, toasted and ground
1 teaspoon coriander seed, toasted and ground
1½ cups/250 g cooked cannellini or other tender white beans (or substitute one 15-ounce/430 g can), rinsed and drained
1 whole egg
¼ cup/25 g thinly sliced scallions, white and green parts
2 tablespoons lightly packed dill leaves, chopped
2 tablespoons lightly packed cilantro leaves, chopped
2 tablespoons lightly packed parsley leaves, chopped
2 garlic cloves, minced or microplaned
1 serrano chile, minced or microplaned
Zest of 1 lemon
1 cup/245 g sour cream
¼ cup/52 g harissa
Grapeseed oil

Coarsely grate the fermented vegetables, sweet potato, and parsnip. Turn the grated vegetables out onto a clean dish towel to absorb any excess liquid, then transfer to a large bowl.

In a separate bowl, combine the rice flour, Parmesan cheese, salt, paprika, caraway, and coriander. In another large bowl, combine the beans and egg and smash with a fork or potato masher until roughly combined. Stir in the grated vegetables, scallions, dill, cilantro, parsley, garlic, chile, and lemon zest; add the rice flour mixture and use your hands or a wooden spoon to mix well. The mixture should feel like damp dough. At this point, it can be held, covered, in the refrigerator for several hours before frying.

Preheat the oven to 200°F/90°C. In a small bowl, swirl together the sour cream and harissa. Line a plate or cooling rack with paper towels.

Coat the bottom of a skillet with about ⅛ inch/3 mm of grapeseed oil and set it over medium-high heat; the oil is ready when a drop of water immediately sizzles and evaporates on contact. Working in batches, shape the fritters into cakes about 3 inches/7.5 cm across and ½ inch/1.25 cm thick and place them in the pan, making sure not to overcrowd the pan so that they will fry up crisp instead of soggy. Immediately lower the heat to medium.

Cook the fritters, undisturbed, until the bottoms are deeply golden and release easily from the pan, 3 to 4 minutes. Flip them and repeat on the other side. Transfer the fritters to the lined plate to drain and place them in the warm oven while you make the next batch. Repeat with the remaining batter, adding a little more oil if necessary. Serve the fritters immediately with the harissa–sour cream sauce.

Fermented Whole Vegetables

This recipe is very flexible. It's a template that allows you to ferment your favorite firm-fleshed vegetables—such as carrots, beets, rutabaga, turnips, small cabbages, sunchokes, celery root, parsnips, green beans, and kohlrabi—in any quantity you desire. The vegetables can be fermented singly or together. If you're using beets with other vegetables, both the brine and the vegetables' exterior will take on a rosy hue. We like to keep a small jar of fermented vegetables in the refrigerator to have ready at a moment's notice.

Vegetables
Water
Kosher salt
Spices and aromatics of choice, such as coriander, cumin, or smoked paprika

Choose as many vegetables as you want to ferment and scrub them clean of dirt. Peel them, if desired, and remove the greens and any bruised spots.

Sterilize a large jar, fermentation crock, or other nonreactive container and a fermentation weight (or use a small dish that fits in the jar). Place the vegetables in the jar and set the jar on a kitchen scale, if you have one. Pour in enough water to completely submerge the vegetables, either keeping track of the amount of water you add by volume, or by subtracting the jar/vegetable weight from the jar/vegetable/water weight. Calculate 3.5 percent of the weight of the water used and measure out that weight of salt (page 99). For instance, if you're using 2 pounds/900 g of vegetables in a 1-gallon/4 L crock, you will likely need about 4 cups/900 g of water and 3 tablespoons plus 1 teaspoon/30 g of kosher salt.

Stir the salt into the jar using a long-handled wooden spoon (or add the salt, cap the jar, and shake it well), mixing until the salt is dissolved. Stir in pickling spices and herbs as desired. Place a weight on top of the vegetables to keep them submerged in the brine. Seal the container, using a lid with an airlock if you have one; if you don't, open the container every few days to release carbon dioxide buildup and check for mold, which can be gently lifted off the ferment.

Place the container in a clean, low-light area with an ambient temperature of 60°F to 68°F/16°C to 20°C until the pickles taste sour, anywhere from 2 to 8 weeks, depending on the size of the vegetables. They will keep indefinitely in the refrigerator.

MAKES ½ POUND or 225 GRAMS

Misozuke

Miso imparts a wonderful umami taste to these Japanese preserved vegetables, one that is very different from the flavor of vegetables fermented in brine. This recipe is designed to be flexible. You can easily double the proportions; just take care to prepare each vegetable separately, since their different densities mean that they won't ferment at the same pace. The miso paste can be reused up to four times. With each subsequent use, the paste becomes looser, due to the liquid the fermenting vegetables release into it. After the fourth reuse, the paste makes a delicious addition to soups, stews, roasted vegetables, or braises.

½ pound/225 g vegetables, such as carrots, garlic, baby turnips, pearl onions, okra, green beans, or radishes
2 cups/550 g red, barley, or other dark miso
¼ cup/60 ml mirin
2 teaspoons red pepper flakes
½ teaspoon grated ginger
6 garlic cloves, grated or finely minced
2 (4-inch/10 cm) pieces of kombu, cut into thin strips

Wash the vegetables thoroughly. You can leave them whole or cut them into spears, rounds, or slices. To ferment garlic, divide the heads into individual cloves, peel them, and trim the root ends. Radish greens can be left intact.

In a small bowl, combine the miso and mirin. Add the red pepper flakes, grated ginger, and garlic.

Spread a layer of the miso mixture on the bottom of a glass or ceramic container large enough to hold all of the ingredients. Layer the prepared vegetables with the kombu strips and remaining miso, making sure that the vegetables are well coated with miso and that the paste covers the top layer. Seal the container with a lid after first pressing down on the vegetables and miso to eliminate any air bubbles.

Store the container in a cool, dark place for a few days to several weeks, depending on how highly fermented you want the vegetables to be. Periodically taste them to see if they've achieved the taste you like best. Longer fermentation will result in a more intense flavor, and denser vegetables require more time. Garlic should be left to ferment for a full month.

When the flavor is to your liking, transfer the vegetables to the refrigerator to slow down the fermentation process. Some people like to rinse the vegetables before serving, but we enjoy the flavor of the miso paste, so we usually just scrape a little bit of it off. Store the vegetables in the refrigerator, where they will keep from 1 to 3 months, depending on the density of the vegetables. As they age, they can lose their snap, but they still taste delicious.

SERVES 2 or 3

Duck Fat Steak Fries

Who doesn't love a good French fry, especially when it's redolent with duck fat? These crisp fries come out of the oven nicely salty from having fermented in brine, so all they need is a fillip of ketchup or barbecue sauce and perhaps a grinding of black pepper.

2 large russet potatoes
Kosher salt
Water
1 clean cabbage leaf or 1 tablespoon yogurt whey or lacto brine (from another ferment)
½ cup / 112 g duck fat
Chopped fresh herbs, for garnish
Freshly ground black pepper (optional), for seasoning

Scrub the potatoes, leaving the skin intact. Cut each potato in half lengthwise and then slice each half into 4 to 6 steak-fry–size wedges.

In a 2-quart / 2 L glass vessel, make a brine by dissolving 2½ tablespoons / 22 g kosher salt in 1 quart / 1 L water. To jumpstart fermentation, add the cabbage leaf (or use 1 tablespoon of yogurt whey or lacto brine). Place the potato wedges upright in the brine, making sure that they are fully covered.

Seal the vessel and leave it to sit at room temperature (68°F to 72°F / 20°C to 22°C) for approximately 5 days, opening and resealing the jar once a day to release carbon dioxide. You'll know the potatoes are ready when the brine appears murky and small bubbles indicate active fermentation. Remove the potato wedges from the brine and leave them to drain on tea towels for at least an hour.

Place a high-sided baking dish in a cold oven and preheat to 425°F / 220°C. Once the baking dish is hot, carefully remove it from the oven and add the duck fat. Return the dish to the oven to let the fat heat for 5 minutes or so. Distribute the potato wedges in the hot fat in a single layer, flipping them a couple of times to make sure that they're thoroughly coated. Return the baking dish to the oven and bake for 30 to 35 minutes, turning the potatoes once halfway through the cooking time for even browning.

Transfer the baked wedges to a bowl and toss with your choice of chopped fresh herbs. Season with freshly ground pepper and serve with ketchup or barbecue sauce, if desired.

MAKES ABOUT 2 QUARTS *or* 2 LITERS

Cauliflower-Turmeric Pickle

*This stunning pickle is popular in both Indonesia and Malaysia, where it goes by the simple name of "yellow pickle" (*acar kuning*), thanks to the color the turmeric lends. Although acar kuning often consists of mixed vegetables, we concentrate on cauliflower here. The cauliflower is brined overnight before being briefly cooked in a thick spice paste. To thicken the paste further, ground nuts are added—in Southeast Asia, oily candlenuts are typically used, but peanuts make a fine substitute. With a flavor that is at once sweet, sour, and spicy, this pickle shines as a topping for rice or as a simple side dish. It also works well as a condiment.*

The brine that the cauliflower has soaked in can be reused for another pickling project, especially to flavor onions or carrots. If you prefer a sweeter taste, add another packed tablespoon of brown sugar and heat the brine until the sugar dissolves.

1¼ cups / 150 g raw peanuts
½ cup / 65 g unhulled sesame seeds
1 large (3-pound / 1.4 kg) cauliflower
1 quart / 1 L distilled white vinegar
2 cups / 480 ml water
1 tablespoon ground turmeric
8½ tablespoons / 76 g kosher salt
6 packed tablespoons / 82 g light brown sugar

SEASONING PASTE
¼ cup / 60 ml grapeseed oil
1½ tablespoons / 22 g shrimp paste
2½ tablespoons / 33 g tamarind paste
5 or 6 large shallots (½ pound / 225 g), halved and thinly sliced into half moons
2 green serrano chiles, seeded, halved, and sliced thinly into half moons
8 large garlic cloves, peeled and minced
1 (2-inch / 15 g knob) fresh turmeric, peeled and grated or finely minced, to equal 1 packed tablespoon
1 (3-inch / 15 g knob) ginger, peeled and grated or finely minced, to equal 2½ packed tablespoons
3 packed tablespoons / 12 g finely grated lemongrass (from 1 small stalk, outer leaves peeled off), or 1 tablespoon lemongrass paste
1 to 2 teaspoons chile powder
¼ cup packed / 52 g light brown sugar
2 tablespoons kosher salt

Preheat the oven to 325°F / 160°C. Place the peanuts on a baking sheet. Their skins should slip off easily as you pick them up; if not, rub the nuts gently with your fingers. Place the sesame seeds on a separate baking sheet. Slide both sheets into the oven and roast for 8 to 12 minutes, until toasted and fragrant. Set aside to cool.

Remove the core of the cauliflower and cut the cauliflower into bite-size florets. You should have about 2 pounds / 900 g of prepared florets.

Fill a large bowl with ice water and set it aside. In a large saucepan, combine the vinegar, water, ground turmeric, salt, and brown sugar and bring to a boil. Working in small batches and keeping the brine at a boil, blanch the florets for 30 to 45 seconds; they should be lightly cooked but still crisp. With a slotted spoon, scoop the florets out of the boiling brine and immediately plunge them into the ice bath to stop their cooking. Repeat with the remaining florets. When all are done, drain them from the ice water and set them aside to dry for 20 minutes or so. Scoop the florets into a clean 2-quart / 2 L canning jar and pour the brine over them. Leave the cauliflower to steep at room temperature for 24 hours, then drain.

In a food processor, pulse the peanuts until they are the size of rice grains; set aside.

Next, make the seasoning paste. In a large sauté pan, heat 2 tablespoons of the oil until shimmering. Stir in the tamarind and shrimp pastes and fry for 2 to 3 minutes, until fragrant. Remove the mixture from the pan and set it aside. Heat the remaining 2 tablespoons of oil in the pan and add the shallots. Cook over medium-low heat for 5 minutes, until they begin to buckle. Then stir in the chiles, garlic, turmeric, ginger, lemongrass, chile powder, brown sugar, salt, and reserved shrimp and tamarind paste. Sauté until the shallots have softened, 6 to 8 minutes. Add the cauliflower to the pan, stirring well to coat the florets with the seasoning paste. Cook for 3 minutes to meld the flavors, then add the ground peanuts and the sesame seeds. Stir to combine, then pack the acar into the 2-quart / 2 L jar and seal it tightly. The acar will keep for 3 months in the refrigerator.

Marinated Mushrooms Two Ways
Paprika-Marinated Mushrooms, Russian-Style Marinated Mushrooms

PAPRIKA-MARINATED MUSHROOMS
MAKES ABOUT 1 PINT / 500 ML

Mushrooms lend themselves especially well to bathing in marinades, which not only help preserve them but give them vibrant flavor. You can pretty much travel the world in marinades by changing the profile of the herbs and spices added to the vinegar-and-oil base; in these recipes we embrace Eastern Europe by leaning in to paprika, garlic, and dill. A further advantage of marinated vegetables relative to true pickles is that they're quick to prepare: you can get these mushrooms from the cutting board to a finishing stint in the refrigerator in about 20 minutes.

Besides having built-in umami, mushrooms are packed with nutrients, making them a healthy food choice. And because mushrooms naturally synthesize vitamin D_2 from the sun's rays, and retain up to 90 percent of it even after cooking, you can boost their nutritional value by placing them in direct sunlight for as little as 20 minutes before you cook them.

Marinated mushrooms are a wonderful addition to salads and charcuterie boards, and we often find ourselves eating them as a snack. Their acidic bite also pairs nicely with steak, sausages, and meaty sandwiches.

- 1 pound / 454 g organic cremini, button, or baby shiitake mushrooms
- 2 tablespoons olive oil
- 1 tablespoon kosher salt
- 3 tablespoons / 45 ml apple cider vinegar
- 2 tablespoons red wine vinegar
- 3 garlic cloves, minced
- 1 tablespoon finely chopped fresh parsley
- 1 tablespoon finely chopped fresh dill
- 1 teaspoon coarsely chopped fresh marjoram
- 4½ teaspoons sweet paprika
- 1½ teaspoons smoked paprika
- ½ teaspoon fennel pollen or ground aniseed
- 1 firmly packed teaspoon brown sugar
- 1 teaspoon onion powder
- Grated zest of 1 lemon
- ½ teaspoon freshly ground black pepper

Preheat the oven to 350°F / 180°C. Brush or rinse the mushrooms and trim the stems flush with the bottoms of the caps. In a large roasting pan, toss the mushrooms with the oil and 1½ teaspoons of the salt to coat them evenly. Roast for about 10 minutes, until the mushrooms are tender and have begun to give off liquid.

In a large mixing bowl, prepare the marinade by combining the apple cider vinegar, red wine vinegar, garlic, parsley, dill, marjoram, sweet paprika, smoked paprika, fennel pollen, brown sugar, onion powder, lemon zest, black pepper, and the remaining 1½ teaspoons of the salt. Mix thoroughly.

Stir the hot mushrooms into the marinade and toss to coat them well. Cover the bowl and place it in the refrigerator for about 2 hours, until the mushrooms are well chilled.

Transfer the mushrooms and their marinade into one or more sterilized ½ pint or 1 pint / 250 ml or 500 ml canning jars. The mushrooms will remain tasty for up to 1 month in the refrigerator. CONTINUED ▸

MARINATED MUSHROOMS TWO WAYS CONTINUED

RUSSIAN-STYLE MARINATED MUSHROOMS

MAKES ABOUT 1½ PINTS / 750 ML

Garlic, onions, and dill predominate in this Russian-style marinade. Because flavorless highly processed sunflower oil won't impart the nuttiness that makes these mushrooms stand out, be sure to use a cold-processed oil.

- 1 pound / 454 g organic cremini or button mushrooms
- ⅔ cup / 160 ml apple cider vinegar, plus a splash for boiling the mushrooms
- 3 tablespoons / 27 g kosher salt, plus a big pinch for boiling the mushrooms
- ⅔ cup / 160 ml cold-pressed sunflower oil
- 1 large onion, thinly sliced into rings
- 2 garlic cloves, minced
- ⅔ cup / 160 ml red wine vinegar
- 1 tablespoon granulated sugar
- 2 bay leaves
- 2 sprigs fresh thyme
- 1 teaspoon whole black peppercorns
- ⅔ cup / 160 ml water
- ¼ cup / 4 g finely chopped fresh dill
- 2 tablespoons finely chopped fresh parsley

Sterilize one or more canning jars with a total capacity of at least 1½ pints / 750 ml. Brush or rinse the mushrooms and trim the stems flush with the bottoms of the caps. If the mushrooms are large, cut them in half or in quarters.

Bring a large pot of water to a boil and season it with a generous splash of apple cider vinegar and a large pinch of salt. Add the mushrooms and return the water to a boil, then cover the pot and boil gently for 2 minutes. Drain the mushrooms in a colander, discarding the water.

In a large pot or skillet, heat 2 tablespoons of the oil over medium heat. Add the onions and garlic to the hot oil and sauté gently until they are translucent and fragrant, about 5 minutes. Pour in the remaining oil, the ⅓ cup / 80 ml of apple cider vinegar, and the red wine vinegar, then add the 1½ tablespoons of salt and the sugar, bay leaves, thyme, and peppercorns. Stir to combine. Add the water and bring the mixture to a simmer. Cook for 3 to 5 minutes to meld the flavors. Add the boiled mushrooms, stirring to coat them well. Remove the pot from the heat.

Leave the mushrooms to cool for about 10 minutes, then stir in the dill and parsley. Transfer the mushrooms and their marinade to the sterilized canning jar(s). The marinade should cover the mushrooms completely; if necessary, add a bit more vinegar or oil. Seal the jars tightly and refrigerate for at least 24 hours before eating. The mushrooms will keep for up to 3 months in the refrigerator.

MAKES 1½ PINTS *or* 750 MILLILITERS

Sambal-Style Chile Pepper Paste

Sambal is a hot pepper paste used throughout Indonesia. At its most basic, this condiment contains nothing more than chile peppers, vinegar, and salt; like curry mixtures, sambal comes in many variations. When served with plain rice, sambal is a classic example of the core-fringe theory, enlivening a bland starch with a piquant accompaniment.

Classic sambals are made by pounding chiles in a mortar and pestle to achieve the best texture and flavor. Sambal can be raw or cooked, with consistencies ranging from near-liquid to a thicker paste. We're partial to thick sambals that have been mellowed by cooking. The fieriness will depend on the chiles you use; take a tiny taste of the hot peppers before adding them to determine how many to include. This sambal is also wonderfully aromatic from galangal and ginger and citrusy from lime.

½ cup / 12 g dried chile peppers, such as chiles de árbol, soaked in warm water until soft
3 whole salt-cured anchovies or 6 fillets (1½ ounces / 43 g)
7 to 10 ounces / 200 to 280 g fresh hot chile peppers, such as serrano or bird's eye
5 ounces / 140 g sweet peppers, such as Corno di Toro or red bell
3½ ounces / 100 g (1 scant cup) peeled and thinly sliced garlic cloves
3½ ounces / 100 g (1 cup) peeled and thinly sliced fresh galangal
3½ ounces / 100 g (1 scant cup) peeled and thinly sliced fresh ginger
3½ ounces / 100 g (2 medium) peeled and thinly sliced shallots
1½ teaspoons ground cumin
1½ teaspoons ground coriander
Zest of 2 limes
3¾ teaspoons kosher salt
1 cup / 240 ml neutral oil, such as grapeseed oil

Soak the dried chiles in warm water until soft, about 30 minutes. Drain and set aside.

Soak the anchovies in cool water for 15 minutes, then drain. If they are whole, remove the backbones. Mince the anchovies finely and set aside.

Remove the stems from the peppers and place them in a food processor. Add the soaked dried chile peppers, anchovies, garlic, galangal, ginger, shallots, cumin, coriander, lime zest, and salt. Pulse all the ingredients to a fairly fine texture; avoid overprocessing them into a smooth paste.

Heat the oil in a wide-bottom pot over medium heat. Carefully scrape the chile paste into the hot oil—it will bubble furiously. Lower the heat to medium-low and cook for 15 to 20 minutes, stirring frequently to avoid scorching. If needed, reduce the heat to low. When the paste is cooked, a thin slick of oil will remain on top.

Leave the paste to cool completely. Sterilize three ½-pint / 250 ml glass canning jars. When the paste is cool, transfer it to the jars. Place a piece of plastic wrap flush against the top of the paste in each jar, pressing down to displace any air and deter mold. Cover the jars with tight-fitting lids. Place them in a clean, low-light area with an ambient temperature of 60°F to 68°F / 16°C to 20°C for 1 week, unscrewing the lids briefly each day to release any built-up carbon dioxide and check for mold, which can be carefully scraped off. Let the paste ferment for 10 to 14 days, or leave it longer for a deeper flavor. Once the paste has fermented to your liking, transfer the jars to the refrigerator, where the paste will keep for well over a year.

MAKES ABOUT 1 QUART *or* 1 LITER

Fire-Roasted and Oil-Preserved Peppers

Peppers of all sorts, both spicy and sweet, are well served by charring. Not only does an open flame create heightened flavor, it makes the peppers' skins easy to remove after they've been left to steam as they cool. The result is a tender vegetable that is ready to eat when seasoned with olive oil, vinegar, and a little salt. Better yet, you can preserve them for months with a little vinegar and enough oil to cover the peppers so that oxygen can't reach them.

Long peppers come in various sizes, sometimes reaching a length of 8 inches/ 20 cm. Since they're so pliable after charring, they can easily be packed into a 1-quart/1 L jar. Smaller peppers will fit into 1-pint/500 ml jars.

These peppers are delicious as part of an antipasto platter, mixed into salads, or as a garnish for meats. Or turn them into a meal by stuffing them with cheese, walnuts, and herbs, as in the recipe that follows this one.

1½ pounds/680 g long sweet or mild chile peppers, such as Marconi or Cubanelle

¾ cup/180 ml red wine vinegar

1 tablespoon kosher salt

1½ cups/360 ml extra-virgin olive oil, plus more as needed to cover the peppers

---

Sterilize one 1-quart/1 L glass canning jar, if you are roasting large peppers, or two 1-pint size/500 ml jars if you are roasting smaller ones.

Preheat a grill or stovetop gas burner to high. Place the whole peppers directly over the flame or on the grill grates and roast them, turning them occasionally with tongs, until the skin is charred and blistered all over. This should take 10 to 15 minutes. Once the peppers are charred, immediately transfer them to a bowl and cover it with plastic wrap or a clean kitchen towel. Leave the peppers to steam for 15 minutes or more to make it easier to remove the skin. When they have cooled enough to handle, gently peel off the skin with your fingers; it should come off easily. Do not rinse the peppers under water; this would remove some of the delicious charred flavor. It's fine if a bit of skin with black flecks remains.

Slice off the tops of the peppers with a knife. Then, using a small spoon, carefully remove the seeds and inner membranes, keeping the peppers whole. Return the peppers to the bowl. Add the vinegar and salt and toss well.

Place large salted peppers and vinegar in the sterilized 1-quart/1 L jar, allowing them to fold over as necessary, or divide small peppers evenly among the two 1-pint/500 ml glass jars. Pour enough olive oil into the jar(s) so the peppers are completely submerged; if not, add enough olive oil to cover them. To rid the jars of air bubbles, place a tea towel on the counter and gently tap the jars on the towel a few times to force any air bubbles to the surface. Seal the jars tightly and store in the refrigerator, where the peppers will last for up to 3 months.

For longer storage, you can process them in a hot-water bath according to the jar manufacturer's instructions. Let the peppers marinate in the oil for at least 1 day before using them to allow the flavors to meld. They will become more flavorful over time.

SERVES 2

Cheese-Stuffed Roasted Peppers

This rich, cheesy filling is a perfect complement to the vinegary preserved peppers on page 71, and the walnuts add a nice crunch. If your peppers are large, this amount of stuffing will fill approximately four of them. If they are very small, you'll have enough filling left over to bake in a pastry shell or in hollowed-out tomatoes.

½ cup / 115 g crumbled feta
⅓ cup / 150 g farmer's cheese
¼ cup / 30 g finely grated Parmesan cheese
1 egg, gently whisked
Scant ½ cup / 45 g walnuts, toasted and chopped into small pieces
1 garlic clove, minced or grated on a microplane
½ serrano or jalapeño chile, minced or grated on a microplane
Zest of ½ lemon
3 tablespoons / 45 ml olive oil
1½ tablespoons finely chopped mint
1½ tablespoons finely chopped parsley
1 tablespoon finely chopped tarragon
1 tablespoon minced chives
¾ teaspoon kosher salt
Freshly ground black pepper, to taste
Fire-Roasted and Oil-Preserved Peppers (page 70), drained and patted dry
Chopped walnuts and fresh herbs of choice, for garnish

Preheat the oven to 350°F / 180°C. In a mixing bowl, combine the crumbled feta, farmer's cheese, Parmesan, egg, walnuts, garlic, chile, lemon zest, olive oil, mint, parsley, tarragon, chives, salt, and pepper. Mix well to combine.

Carefully open each pepper. A piping bag will make stuffing them easier and neater, but you can also use a small spoon. Pipe or spoon the filling into each pepper, packing it tightly without overfilling.

Place the stuffed peppers in a cazuela or other shallow baking dish. Spoon a bit of olive oil over the top. Bake for 20 to 25 minutes, until the peppers and filling are heated through. Before serving, broil for a minute to char the tops lightly and garnish with chopped walnuts and herbs.

MAKES ABOUT 1 QUART *or* 1 LITER

Pickled Cherry Tomatoes

These lustrous pickles are bathed in a spicy, sweet, and sour brine that makes each little orb really pop. Serve them as part of a charcuterie platter, or as an irresistible snack. The longer you leave the tomatoes to pickle, the more flavorful they become.

1 pound/454 g firm but ripe cherry tomatoes
1 cup/240 ml white vinegar
½ cup/120 ml rice vinegar
¼ cup/60 ml mirin
¼ cup/60 ml water
¼ cup/50 g granulated sugar
2½ tablespoons/22 g kosher salt
1 teaspoon whole black peppercorns
1 teaspoon coriander seed
1 teaspoon caraway seed
½ teaspoon red pepper flakes, or to taste
3 garlic cloves, thinly sliced
3 sprigs fresh thyme
3 sprigs fresh dill
2 sprigs fresh basil
1 sprig fresh oregano
1 small red onion, thinly sliced

Wash the cherry tomatoes and prick each one with a push pin or toothpick; this helps the brine penetrate the tomatoes and keeps them from floating to the top of the jar.

In a medium saucepan over low heat, combine the white and rice vinegars, mirin, water, sugar, salt, peppercorns, coriander seed, caraway seed, and red pepper flakes. Bring to a boil, stirring occasionally to dissolve the sugar and salt. Once they have dissolved, remove the pan from the heat and leave the mixture to cool to body temperature.

While the brine is cooling, sterilize one 1-quart/1 L jar or a few smaller ones. Divide the garlic slices, thyme, dill, basil, oregano, and red onion slices evenly among the jars. Then tightly pack the cherry tomatoes into the jars, leaving about 1 inch/2.5 cm at the top.

Once the brine has cooled, carefully pour it over the tomatoes, making sure they are completely covered. You can place a piece of plastic wrap directly on the surface or top the tomatoes with a small sterilized weight to keep them submerged in the liquid. Leave about ½ inch/1.25 cm of headspace at the top of the jar.

Seal the jars with their lids and leave the tomatoes at room temperature to cool completely. Then transfer to the refrigerator to chill for at least 24 hours before consuming. They will last, refrigerated, for up to 3 months.

MAKES 4 to 6 SERVINGS

Pickled Cherry Tomato and Ricotta Tart

Layers of spicy sauce, sweet caramelized onions, creamy, cheesy filling, and vinegary pickled tomatoes come together beautifully in this luxurious tart. We prefer a flaky piecrust—but you could substitute store-bought puff pastry. For the most elegant presentation, choose a shallow tart pan with a removable bottom. The tart tastes best when eaten the same day it is made, but it will last a couple of days in the refrigerator. Simply reheat to crisp the crust and warm the cheese before enjoying it again.

20 ounces / 560 g ricotta
⅓ cup / 40 g rice flour
1½ cups / 100 g finely grated Parmesan cheese
2 eggs
1½ tablespoons extra-virgin olive oil
1½ teaspoons kosher salt
½ teaspoon freshly ground black pepper
¼ cup / 13 g finely chopped dill
Homemade or store-bought dough for 1 (9-inch / 23 cm) pie
1 quart / 1 L Pickled Cherry Tomatoes (page 74)
3 to 4 tablespoons / 45 to 60 g harissa or Ajvar (page 27)
¾ cup / 180 g chopped Caramelized Onions (recipe follows)

The night before you plan to bake the tart, line a fine-mesh strainer or colander with cheesecloth and set it over a bowl. Place the ricotta in the strainer and fold the edges of the cheesecloth over it to cover. Place the strainer and bowl in the refrigerator for at least 8 hours to allow the ricotta to drain (you can save the whey for baking). You should end up with 2 cups / 454 g of drained ricotta.

Place the ricotta in the bowl of a food processor and blitz it with the rice flour, Parmesan cheese, eggs, olive oil, salt, and pepper. Add the dill and pulse just a couple of times to combine without turning the mixture green. Set aside.

Roll out the dough on a floured surface into a circle slightly larger than a 9-inch / 23 cm tart pan, then carefully line the pan with the dough, pressing it into the corners and sides. Trim any excess dough hanging over the edges, but leave enough to form a sturdy edge all the way around the pan. Dock the dough with a fork to keep the crust from puffing up during baking.

Chill the dough in the refrigerator for about 30 minutes. Preheat the oven to the temperature your dough recipe specifies for blind baking. Place a piece of parchment paper flat against the sides and bottom of the crust, then top the parchment with evenly distributed pie weights, dried beans, or uncooked rice.

Blind-bake the crust for 15 to 20 minutes, then remove the parchment and weights. Return the crust to the oven for an additional 10 to 15 minutes, until it is fully baked and the bottom is a pale golden brown. Transfer the baked shell to a rack and leave it to cool completely.

Preheat the oven to 425°F / 220°C. With a slotted spoon, remove the tomatoes from the pickling liquid and drain them on a tea towel. Spread a thin layer of harissa or ajvar over the bottom of the cooled tart shell, then spread on the onions. Top the onions with the ricotta filling, smoothing it with the back of a spoon or an offset spatula. It will come right to the top of the crust. Distribute the tomatoes over the filling in a decorative pattern, either in a tight concentric circle or randomly placed. The tomatoes should cover the top of the tart.

Tent the tart loosely with aluminum foil and bake for 30 minutes. Remove the foil and continued to bake until the cheese is slightly puffed and beginning to bronze, 10 to 15 minutes longer. The filling should feel taut, not wet, when you touch it. Transfer the tart to a rack and leave it to cool for about 15 minutes before slicing.

CARAMELIZED ONIONS
MAKES ABOUT 1 CUP / 240 G

4 large yellow or sweet onions
2 tablespoons olive oil
½ teaspoon kosher salt, plus a pinch more
¼ teaspoon freshly ground black pepper
¼ teaspoon ground coriander
3 packed tablespoons roughly chopped parsley leaves

Peel the onions, then cut them in half vertically. Thinly slice each half into half moons.

Heat the olive oil in a large, heavy-bottom skillet over medium-low heat. Add the sliced onions and ½ teaspoon salt to the pan, stirring to evenly coat the onions with the oil. Reduce the heat to the lowest setting, cover the pan, and cook the onions slowly, stirring occasionally to prevent sticking. It will take 45 to 60 minutes for the onions to sweeten and caramelize. About halfway through the cooking process, add the black pepper and coriander, plus another pinch of salt to help release moisture from the onions. Once the onions have turned a deep brown, remove them from the heat and set aside to cool. Then roughly chop them and stir in the parsley. The onions can be prepared up to 3 days ahead of time and stored in the refrigerator.

MAKES ABOUT 2 QUARTS *or* 2 LITERS

Tomato Water

Keeping up with summer's bounty can be a mad rush. Enter tomato water, the simplest of recipes when you're pressed for time. And it uses an abundance of tomatoes. Although you can crush the tomatoes with salt alone, we suggest adding aromatics to make them even more flavorful. Simply drain the tomatoes overnight in the refrigerator, and the next morning you'll wake up to a rosy liquid that enhances vinaigrettes and Bloody Marys or serves as an excellent base for sauces or soups. We like to freeze it in small batches to have on hand throughout the year. You can turn the strained solids into gazpacho or a quick pasta sauce.

7 pounds / 3.2 kg ripe tomatoes
3 cups / 72 g fresh basil leaves
1 cup / 60 g flat-leaf parsley leaves
4 shallots, thinly sliced
6 garlic cloves, thinly sliced
½ cup / 120 ml white balsamic vinegar or champagne vinegar
1 tablespoon granulated sugar
3 tablespoons / 27 g kosher salt

Line a large, fine-mesh sieve or colander with cheesecloth and place it over a large bowl. Working in batches, combine the tomatoes, herbs, shallots, garlic, vinegar, sugar, and salt in a food processor and pulse until the tomatoes are well crushed but not puréed. Transfer the mixture to the prepared sieve, cover, and refrigerate overnight.

The next day you should have about 2 quarts / 2 L of tomato water, ready to use. Tomato water will keep in the refrigerator for a few days but will last indefinitely when frozen.

TOMATO SYRUP
MAKES ½ TO ¾ CUP / 120 TO 180 ML

This syrup is nothing more than reduced tomato water. It adds an enchanting note to all sorts of cocktails, or try drizzling it over sharp cheese.

2 quarts / 2 L Tomato Water

Place the tomato water in a medium, heavy-bottom saucepan over very low heat and simmer, stirring occasionally, until reduced to ½ to ¾ cup / 120 to 180 ml, about 2 hours. As the reduction nears the finishing point, the bubbles will become very small. Watch closely, as it can quickly burn. The syrup is ready when it coats the back of a spoon. Let it cool completely in the pan, then transfer to a nonreactive, airtight container, where it will last at room temperature for up to 1 year.

MAKES 1½ PINTS *or* 750 MILLILITERS

Green Tomato Marmalade

Unripe green tomatoes have a wonderful acidity that lends itself well to preserves. Here we pair them with plenty of lemon to make a puckery-sweet marmalade with hints of vanilla, cardamom, and thyme. As summer yields to autumn, this is a good way to use up the end-of-season tomatoes that refuse to ripen on the vine.

2¼ pounds / 1 kg green tomatoes
4 organic, unwaxed lemons
1 vanilla bean, split
1 cup plus 6 tablespoons / 285 g granulated sugar
2 tablespoons fresh ginger, peeled and minced
¼ cup / 60 ml dry vermouth
1 tablespoon dried lavender flowers
4 green cardamom pods
2 bay leaves
1 to 2 tablespoons fresh thyme leaves (preferably lemon thyme)

Core the tomatoes and cut them into small pieces, then transfer to a large, nonreactive bowl. Cut 2 of the lemons in half, then seed them and slice them into paper-thin half moons by hand or on a mandoline, and add the lemon slices to the tomatoes. Zest the other 2 lemons, place the zest in airtight container, and refrigerate. Halve the zested lemons, seed them, and squeeze them to yield ¼ cup / 60 ml of juice.

Scrape the vanilla seeds into the tomatoes and drop in the bean. Add the lemon juice, sugar, ginger, vermouth, lavender, cardamom, and bay leaves to the bowl and stir. Leave the mixture to macerate, covered, at room temperature for 12 to 24 hours, so that the sugar draws out the moisture from the tomatoes. Stir occasionally.

When you're ready to proceed, sterilize three ½-pint / 250 ml jelly jars and set them aside.

Pour the macerated mixture into a rondeau pan or large pot with a wide surface area and bring to a boil over medium-high heat. Cook for 20 to 30 minutes, until the jam has thickened and turned shiny; stir often, especially toward the end. The cooking time will depend on the water content and ripeness of the tomatoes. As the mixture boils, use a spoon to gently skim off any foam from the surface to give the jam a clearer finish.

The jam is ready when a spoon swiped across the bottom of the pan leaves a trail before the jam fills it in again (an instant-read thermometer will register 218°F to 221°F / 103°C to 105°C). Remove the vanilla bean, cardamom pods, and bay leaves, then stir in the reserved lemon zest and the thyme leaves.

Remove the pan from the heat and immediately ladle the hot jam into the jars. Cover with lids and let cool to room temperature, then store the jam in the refrigerator for up to 4 months. For longer keeping, you can process the jam in a water bath according to the jar manufacturer's specifications.

MAKES 5 CUPS *or* 1.2 LITERS

Mixed Vegetable Tzimmes

The word tzimmes *in Yiddish means "a fuss" or "a big deal," as in "What's all the fuss about?" or "What's the big deal?" In this classic Ashkenazi dish, the only fuss is the number of ingredients to chop. But the taste is definitely a big deal.*

Tzimmes is traditionally made with some combination of carrots, sweet potatoes, and prunes. It can also be made by cooking the vegetables and fruits with a tough cut of beef, such as flanken, which benefits from hours-long stewing. But since we like our vegetables to be the center of attention, and certainly don't want them to end up overcooked, we stay vegetarian, and roast a variety of vegetables to bring out their sweetness. We then let them sit with dried fruits and honey overnight to develop their flavors before finishing the dish with a quick turn on the stovetop.

The tzimmes will be especially beautiful if you can find yellow beets, both pickled and raw, though the deep red version holds plenty of delight.

- ½ pound / 225 g raw beets
- ½ pound / 225 g carrots
- ½ pound / 225 g sweet potato
- ½ pound / 225 g winter squash, such as honey nut, kabocha, or butternut
- ½ pound / 225 g parsnips
- ¼ pound / 115 g Pickled Beets (page 87, or use store-bought)
- ¼ cup / 60 ml brine from the pickled beets
- ½ cup / 65 g mixed diced dried fruit, such as apricots, pears, and apples
- ½ cup / 165 g mild honey or ½ cup / 107 g packed light brown sugar
- Rind and juice of 1 large lemon
- 2 tablespoons orange juice
- 1 (1-inch / 2.5 cm) knob ginger, peeled and finely grated or minced
- ¼ cup / 60 ml neutral vegetable oil
- 1 tablespoon kosher salt
- ¼ teaspoon freshly ground black pepper
- Chopped fresh parsley, for garnish

Preheat the oven to 425°F / 220°C. Trim and peel the beets, carrots, sweet potatoes, squash, and parsnips. Wrap each type of vegetable individually in foil and roast until tender, 30 minutes to 1 hour, depending on the vegetables. Grate them coarsely in a food processor and transfer to a medium bowl, along with any liquid that may have collected in the foil packets.

Grate the pickled beets and add them to the bowl along with the pickling brine, dried fruit, honey, lemon rind, lemon and orange juices, and ginger. Cover the bowl and leave the mixture to sit overnight at room temperature.

The next day, pour the vegetable oil into a large, wide pan (a 12-inch / 30 cm skillet is ideal) and add the vegetables along with the salt and pepper. Bring to a boil, then reduce the heat to medium-low and cook, stirring frequently to avoid scorching, for 18 to 25 minutes, until nearly all of the liquid has evaporated and the mixture has thickened.

Once the tzimmes has cooled, transfer it to a covered container and store in the refrigerator, where it will keep for 2 months. Serve chilled or at room temperature, garnished with chopped parsley.

MAKES ABOUT 3½ CUPS *or* 650 GRAMS

Beet and Carrot Eingemacht

Eingemacht is a sweet root-vegetable jam, usually prepared for Passover from beets that have been stored over the winter. Most eingemacht recipes call for whopping amounts of beet sugar, which was newly affordable in late nineteenth-century Eastern Europe thanks to the burgeoning sugar-beet industry. We've dialed down the traditional sweetness by adding pickled beets and their brine and substituting honey for granulated sugar, and we include carrots as well. The flavor of eingemacht resembles that of tzimmes, though the dish is less fussy to prepare.

½ pound / 225 g fresh beets
½ pound / 225 g carrots
5 ounces / 140 g Pickled Beets (recipe follows)
½ cup / 120 ml brine from the pickled beets
½ cup / 170 g mild honey
Zest and juice of 1 large lemon
2 tablespoons peeled and grated ginger

Preheat the oven to 425°F / 220°C. Trim and peel the beets and carrots and cut them into large chunks. Wrap them in foil and roast until tender, about 1 hour. Grate them coarsely in a food processor and transfer to a medium bowl, along with any liquid that collected in the foil.

Grate the pickled beets and add them to the bowl along with the pickling brine, honey, lemon zest and juice, and ginger. Cover, and let the mixture sit at room temperature overnight.

The next day, scrape the vegetables into a large, wide pan and bring to a boil over medium-high heat. Reduce the heat to medium-low and cook until almost all of the liquid has evaporated and the mixture has thickened, 10 to 12 minutes.

Transfer the cooled eingemacht to a covered container. It will keep in the refrigerator for at least 3 weeks. Serve chilled or at room temperature.

PICKLED BEETS
MAKES ABOUT 1 QUART / 1 L

2 pounds / 900 g fresh beets
1½ cups / 360 ml apple cider vinegar
½ cup / 120 ml water

7 tablespoons / 90 g sugar
½ cup / 40 g thinly sliced red onion or shallots
2 whole cloves
1¼ teaspoons whole black peppercorns
1 bay leaf
2 tablespoons kosher salt
2 thin slices of peeled fresh horseradish (optional)

Preheat the oven to 425°F / 220°C. Scrub the beets and trim the tops, but leave the root ends intact. Wrap the beets in foil or place them in a covered dish and roast for 30 to 60 minutes, depending on the size of the beets, until a knife slides into them easily. Set them aside to cool.

While the beets are roasting, sterilize a 1-quart / 1 L canning jar. Then place the remaining ingredients in a medium saucepan and bring to a boil. Boil for 2 to 3 minutes, until the sugar and salt have dissolved; set aside.

When the beets are cool enough to handle, slip off the skins and trim any straggling roots. Place them in the sterilized jar.

With a slotted spoon, fish out the onions, cloves, bay leaf, and horseradish from the brine, along with most of the peppercorns; add these to the jar with the beets. If the brine has cooled, reheat it, then pour the hot liquid over the beets to cover. Depending on how the beets are packed in the jar, you may not use all of the brine.

Seal the jar and cool at room temperature, then refrigerate for 3 days before using. The beets will keep for several months in the refrigerator.

MAKES 2 QUARTS *or* 2 LITERS

Dongchimi

Harvested in late fall, the small white Korean radishes known as mu *are the basis of a simple yet elegant winter kimchi called* dongchimi. *Unlike spicy red kimchi, dongchimi is a so-called water kimchi that is fermented in a light brine of water and salt. Though our version derives from the traditional preparation, it provides for a faster ferment, one that does not require burying the kimchi in the ground in special earthenware pots, or onggi.*

The thirteenth-century poet Yi Gyubo is credited with the first written record of kimchi. He likely had dongchimi in mind when he wrote: "Pickled radish slices make a good summer side-dish./Radish preserved in salt is a winter side-dish from start to end./The roots in the earth grow plumper every day,/Harvesting after the frost, a slice cut by a knife tastes like a pear." Dongchimi offers a taste of the fall harvest that lasts throughout the winter—a wonderfully crisp accompaniment to hearty dishes.

Our modern version calls for daikon, as well as Asian pear, Napa cabbage, carrots, and onions for additional flavor and texture. The ferment becomes pleasantly tangy after only a few days, rather than the weeks required for whole radishes. The broth's umami notes add depth to the dongchimi's fizzy brine, which in Korea is sometimes turned into a cold noodle soup in summertime.

---

1 (4-inch by 4-inch/10 cm by 10 cm) piece kombu
2 dried shiitake mushrooms
6 cups/1.4 L cold water
1 pound/454 g daikon, cut into planks 2 inches/5 cm long and ½-inch/ 1.25 cm thick
3 tablespoons/27 g kosher salt

SEASONING PASTE
4 garlic cloves, finely grated or minced
1 tablespoon finely grated ginger
2 teaspoons granulated sugar
3 tablespoons/27 g kosher salt
1 tablespoon soy sauce
1 tablespoon fish sauce
¾ pound/340 g Napa cabbage, cut vertically into 2-inch/5 cm wide pieces
¼ pound/115 g Asian pear or tart apple, peeled, cored, seeded, and julienned
¼ pound/115 g carrots, peeled and julienned
¼ pound/115 g onion, thinly sliced
3 scallions, cut into 2-inch/5 cm pieces

Sterilize a 2-quart/2 L nonreactive jar or crock.

In a saucepan, soak the kombu and dried mushrooms in the cold water for 1 hour, then set over low heat and simmer for 20 minutes. Cool to room temperature.

Meanwhile, place the cut daikon in a large bowl with the salt and leave it to sit for 1 to 2 hours, turning the pieces occasionally.

In another large bowl, make the seasoning paste: combine the garlic, ginger, sugar, salt, soy sauce, and fish sauce. Stir in the cabbage, pear, carrots, onion, and scallions and toss to coat the vegetables evenly. Add the brined daikon and mix well.

Transfer the vegetables to the sterilized jar. Remove and discard the solids and pour the kombu broth over the vegetables. Seal the jar and ferment the vegetables for 2 to 3 days at room temperature, tasting after the second day to determine whether they have fermented to your liking. When they are ready, refrigerate the jar to retard fermentation. The dongchimi will keep for at least 3 months.

MAKES ABOUT 1¼ POUNDS *or* 560 GRAMS

Pumpkin Candy

The Romans often preserved fruits and nuts by candying them in honey. But it was only after the tenth century, when the Arabs introduced sugar to Sicily, that candying evolved into a confectionary art. Even so, the word "candy" hardly brings vegetables to mind. And yet vegetables offer a delightful vehicle for preserving the harvest in a form other than jam.

Pumpkin lends itself especially well to the candying technique. Peeled and cut into chunks, it is parboiled before being immersed in sugar syrup, where it undergoes several sessions of steady boiling, punctuated by periods of rest to enable the sugar to permeate the flesh. If you like candied fruits, you'll love this chewy, slightly sticky treat, which can be nibbled on its own for a quick boost of energy or served alongside a dark chocolate or spice cake.

1½ pounds / 680 g pumpkin, preferably sugar or Cinderella, peeled and scraped free of fibers and seeds

3 tablespoons / 21 g calcium hydroxide powder (see Notes on Ingredients, page 99)

2 quarts / 2 L water

SYRUP

5¼ cups / 1 kg granulated sugar
3½ cups / 840 ml water
¾ cup / 180 ml orange juice without pulp
½ cup / 120 ml freshly squeezed lime juice
1½ tablespoons kosher salt

TO FINISH

3 tablespoons / 23 g confectioners' sugar
3 tablespoons / 24 g cornstarch

Cut the pumpkin into ¾-inch- / 2 cm-thick squares, rectangles, or triangles, making sure not to slice the pieces too thin, as they need sufficient mass to absorb the syrup and achieve a slightly chewy texture.

In a large container, dissolve the calcium hydroxide in the 2 quarts / 2 L of water. Add the pumpkin and leave it to soak overnight at room temperature. The next day, thoroughly rinse the pumpkin. Bring plenty of clean water to a boil in a large pot and par-cook the pumpkin over medium heat for 20 minutes. Drain in a colander and rinse the pieces with cold water.

TO MAKE THE SYRUP: In a high-walled medium saucepan, combine the sugar, water, orange juice, lime juice, and salt and bring to a boil over medium heat. Carefully add the pumpkin and return the syrup to a boil, stirring frequently. Boil the pumpkin for 15 minutes, then turn off the heat, cover the pan, and leave the pumpkin to cool to room temperature. Repeat this step two more times.

Once the syrup has cooled for the third time, bring it to a boil once more and cook the pumpkin at a medium boil until the pieces are completely saturated with the syrup but not falling apart. Depending on the moisture content of the pumpkin, this step can take anywhere from 30 to 90 minutes. Check frequently to make sure there is still plenty of syrup in the pan so that it doesn't burn. Add a bit of boiling water as needed to prevent burning. Once the pumpkin is done, and while the syrup is still hot, drain the syrup into a jar to use in cocktails or as a topping for ice cream or yogurt. The syrup will keep in the refrigerator for up to 3 months. CONTINUED ▶

PUMPKIN CANDY CONTINUED

Preheat the oven to 195°F/90°C. Line a baking tray with parchment paper and distribute the pumpkin pieces in a single layer, leaving a little space between each one. Bake for 2 hours, then flip the pieces and bake for another 30 to 60 minutes, until the surface no longer feels tacky. Leave the pumpkin to cool on the pan.

TO FINISH: Combine the confectioners' sugar and cornstarch in a medium bowl. Once the pumpkin is cool, toss the pieces in this mixture. Store the candied pumpkin in an airtight container, where it will last for 3 to 6 months. It's a good idea to put a couple of desiccant packets in with the candy to keep it from hydrating as it sits in the container.

Homemade Paprika

Although red peppers—capsicums—originated in Central and South America, the finest paprika is associated with Hungary. Turkish invaders introduced the peppers to Hungary in the sixteenth century, and Hungarians have never looked back. Paprika—the deep red spice produced by drying the peppers—is now a defining flavor of Hungarian cuisine. Here, we return paprika closer to its native soil by making the spice at home. Choose any variety of cylindrical red pepper, either sweet or hot, depending on whether you prefer a mild or fiery flavor.

Sweet or hot red peppers, such as Corno di Toro, cayenne, jalapeño, serrano, or biquinho

DRYING PEPPERS IN A DEHYDRATOR

Set the dehydrator to 95°F to 105°F/35°C to 40°C. Slice the peppers in half lengthwise and arrange the pieces on the dehydrator racks with ample spacing for a good airflow. The exact drying time will depend on the size of the peppers and the particular dehydrator. Check them after 48 hours and fairly regularly thereafter; they can take as long as 72 hours to reach the right point. They are ready when they can be crumbled by hand but are not entirely brittle. Be careful not to over-dry them, as this causes essential oils to be lost.

AIR-DRYING PEPPERS

Thread a long sewing needle with twine. With the needle, pierce the flesh near the top of each pepper's stem on two sides and carefully draw the twine through the holes. String the peppers together, making a knot in between each one so that they don't touch. Hang the peppers in a well-ventilated area away from direct sunlight, avoiding temperatures greater than 100°F/38°C. The peppers are ready when they can be crumbled by hand but are not entirely brittle. The drying time generally takes 1 to 2 weeks, depending on how hot and dry the local climate is.

GRINDING DRIED PEPPERS

To make paprika, destem, scrape out the seeds, and grind the dried peppers in a food processor. To make a fine powder, we recommend grinding them again in a spice grinder. It helps to chill the grinder first to prevent heat from affecting the quality of the powder. Store the paprika in an airtight container in a cool, dry space to maintain its quality for up to 1 year.

NOTES ON INGREDIENTS

BARBERRIES These small red berries, similar in size to a currant, have a tart, sour flavor comparable to a cranberry. Frequently used in Persian dishes such as pilafs, dried barberries are easily found online and at Middle Eastern and other specialty shops.

BEETS Several recipes in this volume call for beets as a main or supporting ingredient. You can use red and golden beets interchangeably, despite the difference in color and the golden ones' slightly sweeter taste.

CALCIUM HYDROXIDE Some recipes call for soaking vegetables overnight in a solution of this powder mixed with water before pickling them. Also known as slaked lime, calcium hydroxide ensures that the pickles will remain firm and crisp.

CHILE PEPPERS We use fresh and dried chile peppers throughout this volume to add depth of flavor, heat, and texture. For dried chiles, we favor chiles de árbol, which are on the hotter end of the heat scale. Fresh peppers include jalapeños and the considerably hotter serranos.

DUCK FAT If you don't feel like roasting a whole duck and rendering its fat, packaged duck fat can be purchased at many supermarkets or online. We recommend the D'Artagnan brand.

FENNEL POLLEN This pollen, harvested from blossoms at the tip of the fennel plant in its herbal form, contributes a complex flavor with anise-like notes that give way to a lemony sweetness. Because it is foraged, fennel pollen tends to be expensive; you can substitute toasted and ground aniseed.

GALANGAL This Southeast Asian rhizome is similar to fresh ginger and turmeric, but with citrus notes. It is often used in Thai dishes, such as curries, and is prized for its aromatics and purported health benefits.

HONEY Raw, unpasteurized honey is always our first choice, since it retains the healthful properties that are lost when heated.

MIRIN This Japanese rice wine, used for both cooking and seasoning, adds a subtly sweet flavor.

MISO Most of our recipes call for common white miso, the fermented soybean paste that adds a distinct umami note to any number of dishes, Japanese and otherwise. We also preserve vegetables in red misos, which tend to have a deeper flavor and a bit more salinity than white miso.

OILS We use a range of cooking, marinating, and finishing oils, each of which contributes a different nuance to our recipes. In addition to extra-virgin olive oil, we recommend cold-pressed sunflower oil, pumpkin-seed oil, and grapeseed oil, which has a neutral flavor and a high smoke point that makes it ideal for pan frying.

PAPRIKA We use three different types of paprika, which is made from ground dehydrated red peppers: sweet, hot, and smoked. They are not interchangeable, though if you don't have hot paprika, you can doctor sweet paprika with some cayenne or ground dried chile flakes.

SALT AND SIMPLE BRINE Unless otherwise specified, we use Diamond Crystal Kosher Salt in all of our recipes. To make a simple brine, combine water and salt according to weight, with the salt's weight comprising 3 or 3.5 percent of the water's weight. The math is fairly simple using either standard American or metric measures, since 1 fluid ounce of water weighs just about 1 ounce, and 1 milliliter of water weighs 1 gram. So, for example, to make a 3 percent brine: each 2 cups of water is 16 ounces by weight, so would need a scant ½ ounce of kosher salt by weight, or about 2½ teaspoons; each 500 ml of water is 500 g by weight, and would need 15 g of salt. Scale up as needed.

TAHINI This Middle Eastern paste, made from hulled, ground sesame seeds, delivers a nutty flavor and creamy texture.

NOTES ON EQUIPMENT

BLENDER A countertop blender is not essential for the recipes in this volume, though a few recipes specifically call for one. A blender will yield a silkier purée than a food processor, but in most cases a food processor can substitute.

CANNING JARS AND GLASS VESSELS Several of the recipes in this book require a 1-pint/500 ml glass canning jar with a metal lid for fermentation and storage. Other recipes call for storage in ½-pint/250 ml and 1-quart/1 L jars, as well as a 2-quart/2 L glass vessel, and a 1-gallon/4 L crock for large quantities. It's best to stock up on these vessels before starting projects; packages of 6, 12, and 24 jars are usually available.

CAZUELA A cazuela is a round, shallow earthenware dish commonly used in Spanish, Mexican, and South American cooking. A shallow ceramic or glass baking dish is a fine substitute.

CHEESECLOTH Used for straining, cheesecloth is essential to have on hand for preservation recipes.

FERMENTATION CROCKS Many contemporary crocks are specially designed with airlocks for ease in releasing carbon dioxide buildup during the fermentation process.

FOOD PROCESSOR For recipes that call for shredding, pulsing, and grinding, it helps to have a good food processor within reach—especially one with multiple blade options, including a thin slicing disc. A food processor can also be used in place of a blender if necessary, although the final texture of the food won't be quite as fine.

HEAVY-BOTTOM, NONREACTIVE PANS Some preservation recipes call for a long, slow simmer. A sturdy, nonreactive pan (such as one made from heavy stainless steel) won't react with high-acid foods and will keep ingredients from scorching.

FINE-MESH SIEVE OR STRAINER A well-made fine-mesh sieve or strainer is essential, especially when a recipe calls for draining or pressing on solids to extract all their liquid.

KITCHEN SCALE As in baking, preservation recipes work best when recipe amounts are strictly followed. Weighing ingredients on a kitchen scale ensures consistency. It's useful to have one that measures both ounces and grams.

MANDOLINE While a very sharp knife will usually do, a mandoline allows for quick, ultra-thin slicing or shredding.

MICROPLANE GRATER We use this simple handheld tool to grate garlic and chile peppers and to zest lemons.

MIXING BOWLS Many of our recipes call for temporarily storing prepared ingredients in bowls of various sizes. A nesting set of high-quality glass bowls will come in handy.

PARCHMENT PAPER This smooth, greaseproof paper is used in both baking and cooking to keep foods from sticking to the bottom of a dish or sheet pan.

SLOTTED SPOON We always have a stainless-steel slotted spoon on hand for removing solid ingredients from liquids.

SPICE GRINDER Grinding whole seeds and spices allows cooks to achieve deeper flavors than are possible with previously ground spices, so we recommend using a small, affordable countertop device. Grinding by hand in a mortar and pestle is more old-school but completely acceptable.

INDEX

A
Ajvar, 27–28
Apple Kraut, 14
Asparagus Pickles, Zesty, 33

B
Baba Ghanoush, Charred, 21
barberries, 99
    Carrot and Barbery Salad, 16–17
    Pickled Barberries, 17
beans
    Vegetable Fritters, 52
    Warm Corn Relish, 42–44
beets, 2, 99
    Beet and Carrot Eingemacht, 87
    Mixed Vegetable Tzimmes, 84
    Pickled Beets, 87
    Vinegret, 48–51
brine, 99–100
Brussels sprouts
    Vinegret, 48–51

C
cabbage
    Dongchimi, 88
    Golden Cabbage, 11
    See also sauerkraut
calcium hydroxide, 99
Candy, Pumpkin, 91–92
carrots
    Beet and Carrot Eingemacht, 87
    Carrot and Barberry Salad, 16–17
    Dongchimi, 88
    Mixed Vegetable Tzimmes, 84
    Pickled Carrots, 16–17
    Vinegret, 48–51
Cauliflower-Turmeric Pickle, 60–61
cheese
    Cheese-Stuffed Roasted Peppers, 73
    Pickled Cherry Tomato and Ricotta Tart, 76–77
    Vegetable Fritters, 52

corn
    Sweet Corn Tea, 47
    Tangy Corn on the Cob, 41
    Warm Corn Relish, 42–44
cucumbers
    Cucumbers Brined in a Pumpkin, 34–37
    Pickled Gazpacho with Charred Tomatoes and Peppers, 38
    Vinegret, 48–51

D
daikon
    Dongchimi, 88
    Golden Cabbage, 11
Dongchimi, 88
duck fat, 99
    Duck Fat Steak Fries, 58

E
eggplant
    Ajvar, 27–28
    Charred Baba Ghanoush, 21
    Eggplant Makdous, 25–26
    Fermented Eggplant, 22
Eingemacht, Beet and Carrot, 87
equipment, 101

F
fennel pollen, 99
Fritters, Vegetable, 52

G
galangal, 99
Gazpacho, Pickled, with Charred Tomatoes and Peppers, 38

H
honey, 99

I
indigo, 30–31

M
Makdous, Eggplant, 25–26
Marmalade, Green Tomato, 83
mirin, 99
miso, 99
    Misozuke, 57
mushrooms
    Paprika-Marinated Mushrooms, 65
    Russian-Style Marinated Mushrooms, 66
    Sauerkraut Soup, 12–14

O
oils, 99
Onions, Caramelized, 77

P
paprika, 99
    Homemade Paprika, 95
    Paprika-Marinated Mushrooms, 65
peppers, 99
    Ajvar, 27–28
    Cheese-Stuffed Roasted Peppers, 73
    Eggplant Makdous, 25–26
    Fire-Roasted and Oil-Preserved Peppers, 70
    Golden Cabbage, 11
    Homemade Paprika, 95
    Pickled Gazpacho with Charred Tomatoes and Peppers, 38
    Sambal-Style Chile Pepper Paste, 69
    Sauerkraut Soup, 12–14
    Warm Corn Relish, 42–44
pork
    Sauerkraut Soup, 12–14
potatoes
    Duck Fat Steak Fries, 58
    Vinegret, 48–51
pumpkin
    Cucumbers Brined in a Pumpkin, 34–37
    Pumpkin Candy, 91–92

R
Russian-Style Marinated Mushrooms, 66

S
salad dressings
    Creamy Dressing, 51
    Shallot Vinaigrette, 50
    Spicy Sesame Dressing, 17
salads
    Carrot and Barberry Salad, 16–17
    Vinegret, 48–51
salt, 99
Sambal-Style Chile Pepper Paste, 69
sauerkraut
    Apple Kraut, 14
    Sauerkraut Powder, 14
    Sauerkraut Soup, 12–14

sausage
    Sauerkraut Soup, 12–14
Sesame Dressing, Spicy, 17
Shallot Vinaigrette, 50
soups
    Pickled Gazpacho with
        Charred Tomatoes and
        Peppers, 38
    Sauerkraut Soup, 12–14
squash, 1–2
    Butternut Squash and
        Sesame Purée, 7
    Fermented Winter Squash, 8
    Mixed Vegetable Tzimmes, 84
    Warm Corn Relish, 42–44
Sunflower Seeds, Toasted, 50

T
tahini, 100
**Tart, Pickled Cherry Tomato and
    Ricotta, 76–77**
Tea, Sweet Corn, 47
tomatoes
    Green Tomato Marmalade, 83
    Pickled Cherry Tomato and
        Ricotta Tart, 76–77
    Pickled Cherry Tomatoes, 74
    Pickled Gazpacho with
        Charred Tomatoes and
        Peppers, 38
    Sauerkraut Soup, 12–14
    Tomato Syrup, 80
    Tomato Water, 80
Tzimmes, Mixed Vegetable, 84

V
vegetables
    Fermented Whole
        Vegetables, 53
    health and, 2
    history of, 1–2
    importance of, 2
    Misozuke, 57
    Mixed Vegetable Tzimmes, 84
    transformative power of, 1–2
    Vegetable Fritters, 52
    Vinegret, 48–51
    See also individual vegetables
Vinaigrette, Shallot, 50
Vinegret, 48–51

ACKNOWLEDGMENTS

DARRA GOLDSTEIN

Thanks first to Cortney and Richard, my friends and coauthors. We enjoyed a dream team for this series, helmed by our visionary editor, Jenny Wapner, with whom it's always a joy to work. I'm also thrilled to be working again with another dear friend, designer Frances Baca, who has brought the books to such vivid life. It was great fun working with photographer David Malosh, whose gorgeous photos grace these books, and prop stylist Paige Hicks. Thanks, too, to my agent, Angela Miller, and to Carolyn Insley for guiding the books through production. And finally, I'm grateful for the unfailing support of my sister, Ardath Weaver, and that of my husband, Dean Crawford—for his math genius, his editing, and his endless enthusiasm for new tastes.

CORTNEY BURNS

In gratitude for the time-honored preservation traditions that inspire and enliven our creativity. Thanks to my family for putting up with the plethora of jars and experiments that line our kitchen, and for tasting new and different flavors with wonderment and surprise. To my amazing collaboration team, Darra & Richard; what fun it is to create with you both. I am forever grateful to my literary agent Katherine Cowles, and to all the microbes that make this possible; we humbly thank you!

RICHARD MARTIN

I would like to thank my wife, Sonja, and children Apolline and Loic, for taste testing and allowing my preservation experiments to take over the kitchen for long stretches of time. Thanks also to my extended family: Jan and John, Lee and Lisa, Greg and Patty, and Maddi and Max. Over the years, as a website and magazine editor, I've worked with many inspiring chefs, writers, and friends who expanded my culinary world—thanks to all of you. And to Darra and Cortney, thank you for developing these incredible recipes and allowing us to share them with the world.

Hardie Grant North America
2912 Telegraph Ave
Berkeley, CA 94705
hardiegrantusa.com

Text © 2024 by Darra Goldstein, Cortney Burns, and Richard Martin

Photographs © 2024 by David Malosh

Illustrations © 2024 by Sarah Mafféïs

Photograph page 30 by Aya Brackett

All rights reserved. No part of this book may be reproduced in any form without written permission from the publisher.

Published in the United States by Hardie Grant North America, an imprint of Hardie Grant Publishing Pty Ltd.

Library of Congress Cataloging-in-Publication Data is available upon request

ISBN: 9781958417157
ISBN: 9781958417164 (eBook)

Printed in China
Design by Frances Baca
Prop styling by Paige Hicks

MIX
Paper | Supporting responsible forestry
FSC
www.fsc.org FSC® C020056

FIRST EDITION

NORTH AMERICA

ABOUT THE AUTHORS

DARRA GOLDSTEIN the founding editor of *Gastronomica*, is the author of six award-winning cookbooks, including *Beyond the North Wind: Russia in Recipes and Lore,* named one of 2020's best cookbooks by *Forbes.com, Esquire*, and the *Washington Post*. In 2020 she was honored with the Lifetime Achievement Award from the International Association of Culinary Professionals.

CORTNEY BURNS (with chef Nick Balla) built a larder-based kitchen at San Francisco's Bar Tartine; their cookbook *Bar Tartine* won awards from both the James Beard Foundation and IACP. *Bon Appétit* has dubbed her the "godmother of fermentation" for her modern take on ancient techniques.

RICHARD MARTIN is a media executive, lifestyle editor, and writer who started magazines and websites that have grown into major media companies, including *Complex, Modern Luxury* (Manhattan and Miami), and *Food Republic*.